I0201276

Why Blame Adam and Eve?

How We Did It to Ourselves

Robert E. Joyce

Published by

LifeCom

St. Cloud, Minnesota, USA

© 2014   Robert E. Joyce

All rights reserved

ISBN   978-0-578-14701-7

No part of this book may be used or reproduced in any manner whatsoever without written permission. No part of this book may be stored in a retrieval system or transmitted in any form or by any means including electronic, electrostatic, magnetic tape, mechanical, photocopying, recording or otherwise without the prior permission of the publisher.

For information, address *LifeCom*, Box 1832, St. Cloud, MN 56302

Contents

WHY Do Bad Things Happen to Everyone?

We blame Adam.
Adam blamed Eve.

Eve blamed the Serpent.
And the Serpent blamed God.

Are we blaming the right persons?

Are we satisfied with the imperfect way
we live in the world of the blame chain?

If not, can we become aware of something
that we ourselves are responsible for, but do
not want to know about, preferring to blame
our first parents, and secretly even God?

Preface

From the beginning of human life on planet earth, real joy has been ever-fragile. Our gladness is stabbed by pain, grief, and sorrow. Something is wrong deep within our human hearts. And we weave the meaning of our wounded joy by threads of blaming others.

We know we are headed for an exit from this world. Often we feel insecure about what happens after we die. And we are unconsciously begging to know more about *how* we came to *be, and to be here.* In *this* kind of world, rather than in some other kind.

Our being created out of nothing "set the stage." We might ask, why were we even created to be at all? And when created, did we *receive* our own being, or were we clunked with it? Why do we now lead a precarious life, teetering on the precipice of sickness, trauma, and the destruction of bodily life? And did Adam really *do* this to us? Did Adam and Eve put us here? Whereas, if they had no existence or had not sinned, would we be in a different world?

Sacred Scripture as a whole reveals much about *how* to suffer and what will happen to our mortal bodies and immortal souls. Nevertheless, the mystery of our history is itself swimming in the vast ocean of truth that is still to be revealed.

Our unstable existence is not a problem or a puzzle to be solved, but a mystery to be lived every day. We are then able to understand ever more about the deeper meaning of our mysteries. Electricity, meteorology, and hydration, for instance, are mysteries in which we participate. So, also, are the mysteries of *being created out of nothing and of facing the origin of evil.* But the more we know the mystery, the more we come to know how much we do not know. Yet, we are still knowing more and better than before.

For instance, the more we know about various forms of energy, the more our living will become enriched with the truth about our natural environment and about interactions among ourselves.

Similarly, the more we know about God and the more we willingly admit the sinfulness that is numbing us, the more we can live in humility and truth. We can confront our pride and an unrecognized error about our destiny. Even as we struggle within the present world, we can know more about this world *and* the next. In our conscious life, and as well *in our unconscious life*, the mystery can be opened wider and deeper.

This little book is intended, then, to stimulate wonder and help to increase the desire to deepen our lives—to live with deeper roots. We can come closer to union with everyone and everything around us and beyond us. We can learn how to be friendly with snowflakes and snapdragons, as well as persons. We can become friends even with divine Persons, in the community of the natural and the supernatural.

There is great joy in knowing *all* being. At every moment, we are finitely "in touch," with everyone and everything that *is*. Knowing the vast ocean of reality is an 'unaware' kind of knowing. But that is why we *can* become aware of it. Because even though we do not *think* about it, we already know it unconsciously.

If we do not know God and all created reality now, unconsciously, we would have no basis on which to develop this knowing into conscious thought and knowledge. We can expand our minds and hearts even beyond our cherished images and dreams. The story of our origins within Adam and Eve can be realized and reverenced through a broader and more intense light.

There is nothing in this book's message that goes against traditional teaching on creation and the origin of evil. But I seriously request those who revere the traditional religious meaning to consider the grander prospect. And it is this. Truth, revealed within Sacred Scripture and tradition, can be *received* better than ever. The very same truths can be understood at much deeper levels. The meaning of creation out of nothing, for instance, is deeper than the idea of being 'drawn from the dust of the earth.' And the meaning of an original sin is deeper than disobedience in the Garden.

We need to bring personally-enriched minds to the endowment of Revelation. Such improvement would enable us to love God more and to love our neighbors as we love ourselves. Love, without much knowledge, remains weak. The better we understand one another and God, the greater our possibility, here and now, for authentically loving God. After all, we must have been created *out of nothing* to be perfect beings by God's infinitely powerful love.

We can begin forming a better foundation for loving and knowing by seeing everyone and everything, first of all, within the perspective of *being*. We can view all persons and things in their very *acts* of *be*-ing. Not just by observing them in their acts of talk-ing and walk-ing, know-ing and grow-ing, but in their acts of *be*-ing.

Be-ing is our most important act. All other acts stem from our act of *be*-ing, and flow from it.

Let's look at the act of *be*-ing of whatever we are seeing. Insight into *be*-ing takes freely into account the *being* of blades of grass and of microbes, along with the *being* of angels and of God. Everything that *is* we can consider as real being. And we can see that every single being *as a being* has, at least, one thing in common with *all* others. It *is*. *Really*. It is not nothing.

God *is*. And so is a speck of dust. Both manners of being really *are*. They may be infinitely diverse with respect to their *kind* of *being*, that is, in their *essence* and in their significance for us. God, for instance, is eternal. Dust, water drops, snowflakes, and the like are fleetingly temporal. God and creatures are *infinitely* different in *kind* of being, but they are *all*, in common, really *be*-ing their being. This fresh perspective on the *miracle of being and of being-at-all* can be acquired by us, if we sincerely *desire* to see. After all, we ourselves are *be*-ing our being, right at this moment, whether we desire to do so or not. We are *be*-ing our own being, and not that of anyone else.

The contemporary world is filled with gnostic strains produced by those who would willingly turn away from historically-rooted divine Revelation. Escapist theories abound, for instance, in what some call "new age." The reader can be sure that there is nothing in this book that is gnostic or elitist. Everything is accessible to those who are willing to wonder and to be faithful to their reason, as they think about their faith. The key truths we will consider are neither new age nor old age: most are ageless—timeless and spaceless.

The book takes a strong stand, between two opposing theological deviances. On the one side, historically, there is pantheism, wherein everything is ultimately thought to be God. On the other side, there is deism, where people think that God sets the world in motion and goes AWOL. I stand in the midst of the stream of contemplative thought that is found in the teachings of historic Christianity, and most particularly the Catholic Church. But I am writing for all who sincerely seek deeper meaning for their faith or for those who desire to believe.

So, who is willing to *wonder*? Seriously. Especially, within the world of ceaseless distractions containing entertainments 24/7, electronic gadgets galore, and the whirligig of hyperactivity. Wonder does not mean figuring things out or the planning of agenda. Wonder requires the *desire to unite* with the truth in everyone and in everything—not simply to conform to what is. A genuine understanding and wisdom *begins only* in those who are willing to wonder and to act with *love for truth, and not simply for ego gratification or out of defensiveness about past or present positions.* Wisdom can come only to the degree that we willingly wonder.

The reader is encouraged to develop an ever-deeper understanding of who we are, why we are here, where we are headed, and with what kind of attitude.

Further reading can be found in my larger works on the subject of creation and the origin of evil. A listing is found at the end of this book.

Please feel free to communicate your response to this book by email. I seek remarks of agreement, as well as challenge. Simple, serious questions are welcome.

Robert E. Joyce, PhD
July 15, 2014
robertjoyce@charter.net
Lifemeaning.com

Introduction

The Elephant in the Believing Room

The believing room for Jews, Christians, and others stands massive, magnificently meaningful, and stunningly beautiful. But, lurking in the shadows, there lives an immense elephant. So far, within human history, the existence of this incredible presence is being overlooked and denied, unconsciously and chronically, even by those with faith in divine Revelation.

In front of the huge shadowy stalker, the figures of Adam and Eve parade themselves, back and forth, with myriad pageantry. Their story is repeated endlessly. People have become fixed on it. How God created Adam out of the dust of the earth and Eve from his rib; how they enjoyed the gifts of Eden; and how they were tempted, fallen, and banished.

Few of those listening wonder about the context for this drama of creation and sin. And fewer dare to think that perhaps the scenes in the Garden of Eden are not the *very* beginning of the human story— that there is a deeper beginning, exceedingly more glorious, and also profoundly heartbreaking.

Jews, Christians, and others believe that God's goodness, power, and freedom are unlimited. Most might declare that divine love for Adam and Eve and for all of us personally is, of course, unlimited.

But, if so, the original love of God cannot be told by the *Genesis* story alone. Why not? That story does not begin at the authentic beginning. It says nothing of the *creation* of the angels. And it overlooks something important about the *being* of human persons.

This Biblical account seems most concerned about the *origin of our fallen* condition. Not about the beginning of our being *out of nothing*. In other words, as an account of events, *Genesis* is not meant to answer all questions. It leaves us with an elephant in the room of our faith. We are looking right at it and not seeing it. The story of Adam and Eve is about the *being* of each one of us, more than about something that happened in space and time.

God's infinite love created us *personally* and *immediately* out of nothing. But, when God said, "Be," what did we say? If we had said fully "No," where would we be? If we had said fully "Yes," where would we be? Surely not in this *fallen world* of "Maybe." Maybe I will live another year or another day. Maybe tomorrow the world will blow up for me and for all in this contingent world of space and time.

Here every event and even our very breath appears unnecessary and seems to come by chance. No one can be absolutely certain of anything in our world. God, therefore, could not have put us in this condition, without our "cooperation"—our unwillingness to be the perfect being we were created to be. Our immediate reply to God's gift of being must have been, "Maybe" (*yes/no*).

Our *personally originative* sins, together with those of Adam, Eve, and multitudes who sinned at that moment of the first creation, seem to be too astounding to admit. Whoever has heard of sin at this personally poignant level, buried in our spiritually unconscious life?

The elephant in our believing room is the result of a first failure—the failure to receive our being, freely and fully, at the moment of being created *out of nothing*. The book, *Why Blame Adam and Eve?* allows us to begin hearing a first trumpeting from this wounded, long-starved behemoth.

Chapter 1

When God Said "Be," What Did *We* Say?

Were we created out of nothing as a single cell in the darkness of our mother's body? And without her even knowing that we were there? Is that how God originally creates and relates to a person in the divine image and likeness? Were we simply dropped into being without a word from God or from us?

We did go through a process. It happened. But let us look at the whole thing with a more wondering awareness.

If you believe that God is three infinite Persons, could these Persons be *that* impersonal? Not even allowing us to respond immediately to the gift of creation by exclaiming with the heart of our being, "Thank you for this gift that I *am*"?

Tragically, all of Christian and Jewish understanding of creation labors under one curious *assumption.* We subconsciously assume that God's creating us *out of nothing* could *not* be an activity that is *inter*personal.

We think that God's act of creating us must have been personal on the part of God, who was doing the act. But not on our part. We think our *first* manner of being was to be *out of dust or out of evolution*, and not fresh out of nothing with nothing pre-existing needed. But is that how God creates *persons*?

Before God acted, of course, we did not *be* at all. But we seem to take it for granted that God, who is infinite love, did not infinitely intend us to respond immediately and freely to the gift of our *being*. Do you really think that God did not *infinitely intend* our immediate response of love? That God could not or did not create us able to enter freely, at once, into heavenly union?

This issue remains monumental: *whether or not we were fully free as persons to respond at once to the gift of being.* But what else could we be, except fully free? If we do think otherwise, we shortchange the meaning of our being and of God's *unlimited love for each one of us*—loving us within the divine act of creation. The interpretations of traditional theology and philosophy have been inadequate for understanding what was involved in our creation out of nothing. The deeper significance of divine Revelation concerning creation and the origin of evil is yet to be recognized theologically by the sacred tradition. The truth is ever-present, but it is not consciously being received.

How could creation *out of nothing* be other than immediately *interpersonal*? From three Infinite Persons can we expect *any* act at all that is not *infinitely* interpersonal? God's act of creation could be nothing other than interpersonal—and *only* interpersonal, both on God's side and on our side. The act of calling us to *be as persons*—beings who are angelic and human—would have to be *interpersonal* and super-intimate. *It had to be like no intimacy that you or I have ever experienced or imagined in space and time.* The intimacies of earthly being would have to be considered almost trivial compared to our immediate presence to infinite Love as we were being gifted with being. Otherwise, God is not *God*, but a mega-*creature*.

Do we think that the three divine Persons, gifting us to be and to be preciously personal and immortal, acted less than interpersonally with us? Treated us as somewhat less than real persons? Were they not expecting our fully free and immediate response by virtue of the perfect freedom-power gifted to us? No, their act of gifting us to be must have fully empowered our immediate (finite) response. They could not have created us, for instance, within our mothers, *without first* relating with us immediately, Persons-to-person.

Are we not *persons*, beings with the power to know and to love (intellect and will), who are created originatively right within the heart of *unlimited love*? Every created person as a person is a *receiver* of being: originally a conscious receiver—human persons included. If we have the slightest doubt, perhaps we are denying unconsciously that God gifted us to be perfect, finite beings and that we, immediately and freely, must have received our own being quite imperfectly. We are denying that God is *both* infinitely good *and* infinitely powerful. We do not think that God can and did gift us with *our own ability to love God immediately and freely forever at the moment of creation.* If we do not think so, then, right at this moment, we are personally engaged in an activity of spiritual repression. We *keep ourselves from knowing consciously how* we responded to being created out of nothing. We do not really want to know *why* we are in this kind of world, instead of being united with God in heaven, from the beginning—without having to enter this struggling world at all.

Blinded by the Cosmos

For many centuries, theologians have rightly devoted awesome attention to redemption and salvation. But relatively little effort has been made to understand creation *out of nothing*. In recent times, they have sparred heatedly over creationism and theistic evolution. But neither of the opposing sets of theories treats creation as an *interpersonal* event.

On the one hand, creationists think that God created darkness before the light. He created stones, plants, and animals before human *persons*. And human *persons* were created ages of time after the angels. On the other hand, theistic evolutionists think that God started with primitive matter or a big bang and only quite gradually came to shepherd subpersonal creation into some kind of personal creatures, often called "rational animals."

In any case, with theories like these, virtually no concentration has been devoted to creation *ex nihilo* (creation *out of nothing*) *as necessarily interpersonal*—a case of an immediate "God said, we said."

Yet creation is the beginning of all other beginnings. Knowing what happened at the moment of creation *out of nothing* is critical to understanding the act of God and the act of every creature resulting from it. It is especially important to know *how* we responded to God's gift of our being. We do not realize that we must have had a supremely free *be*-ginning that was similar to, but different from the angels, and *nothing like* our origin on earth.

We have deeply repressed our original act of freedom done at the moment of creation out of nothing. We are massively in denial—unconsciously. We need to become aware of how we must have hidden, from ourselves, that original response to God out of nothing. That response must have been an act abusive of our God-gifted, perfect freedom. We could have said *fully yes* to being-*at-all* and, as well, *fully yes* to being-*who*-we-are. Instead, we must have really hesitated, saying, a kind of *yes/no*—in effect, *maybe*.

Once we can admit our first personal sin against the gift of our freedom, then we can better appreciate how God responded to us by becoming flesh. Christians believe that Jesus identified with us in every way, except sin and the ability to sin, in order to bring us to salvation, *if we are willing. Willing,* not wanting. Everybody *wants* "salvation."

God's creating out of nothing did not happen in or with time and space. Nor did it cause time and space to *be.* Time and space are *imperfect kinds* of being and could not have been created *out of nothing* by an infinitely perfect Creator. These dimensions of existence must have accompanied creation out of something (*ex aliquo*)—creation out of something crashed or imperfect, as in the story of *Genesis.*

A Contradiction?

Theologians still do not seem to understand how they are locked into the spatiotemporal perspective. If they even thought about it, they would presume, for instance, that God creating us and, in the very same instant, we responding would be a contradiction. But that would be true only if the "creator" were an imperfect person. In such case, there would necessarily be an interval of duration, however slight, before the responding act could occur.

But not so with God. *Infinite power* to cause is able to give *being* to the created person and to receive the response in the very same instant—an instant of *perfect freedom* for both infinite and finite beings. There is *no duration at all* in creation out of *nothing.* God alone initiates the creating act, while receiving, with infinite grace, the *immediately free* response. God's *infinite reception* of our first, fully-free response demands immediacy. God is subject to space, time, and duration only in redeeming. Not in creating.

Yet, in viewing creation *out of nothing* (*ex nihilo*), theologians and philosophers *unconsciously* keep God within the narrow frame of temporal dimensions. They do not seem to realize how the *infinite* act of *causing* us to *be* is profoundly different from our finite acts of causing our effects in the present world. They do not recognize clearly how infinite causing is different from finite causing. They seem to overlook how creation out of *nothing* had to be *solely* an activity of *infinite* perfection. God's acts are not bound by our finite and defective world, nor by our usually shortsighted manner of thinking.

For us who are now living in the cosmos, it is impossible to act immediately without space and time being involved in our giving and our receiving. But God is not at all subject to our spatiotemporal existence and its emphatically either/or logic. God is not a kind of finite cause, magnified by our limited minds.

Divine power does both. God both *gives* us our act of *be*-ing and *receives* our *response* at the same spiritual (non-temporal) moment. God *empowers* us directly and immediately to be (finitely) perfect in being and freedom, and to make our own immediately personal response that, if fully positive, would enter us into heavenly union forever.

We need to realize firmly that both infinite and finite giving and receiving are essentially not subject to time or duration. In order for that insight to spread widely, the meaning of analogy and the logic of paradox must continue to develop. Divine giving *and receiving* are purely spiritual, infinite acts done solely for our good. Similarly, *our* acts of finite receiving are likewise *immediate*. They are called to be perfect acts of worship—free, immediate, and forever.

Genesis and the Fire Chief

The *Book of Genesis* is commonly read as though it were reporting the original creation out of nothing. Instead, it should be read as accounting for a creation that is recuperating from a prior fall in our *response* to the gift of *be*-ing. Whether the text is taken literally or symbolically or partially both, the wording obviously intends to represent creation that is *not ex nihilo* (*not* out of *nothing*). It is a creation that is *ex aliquo* (out of *something*: darkness, dust, a rib, and such). That distinction between God's creating out of nothing and God's creating out of something, however, is rarely, if ever, made theologically.

When it comes to understanding the *roots of our sinful condition*, theologians seem to be blocked. How could an infinitely good and infinitely powerful God allow persons who are perfectly innocent to be afflicted with the sin of their first parents? This affliction, so widely understood to be basic truth, is incredibly weak as interpreted so far. And it does little to explain *adequately* the disposition of infinite Love taking on flesh in redeeming us and becoming our Savior.

Does God play games? The idea that we have passively inherited Adam's sin is like claiming that the Fire Chief of your city planned to let some hired arsonists burn your house down, yet also planned to save you from the flames by a rescue at the last minute.

But God did not send the beloved Son to save us from having been *done in* by the sin of others, especially our first parents, *without us also having been implicated* in the origin of the whole predicament. We think of traditional scenarios because we are cosmo-locked: fixated on our space-time condition, as though it were the only condition we could ever have been in. We are intemperately bent on projecting a spatiotemporal framework where it does not belong at all.

Why were we even conceived within the cosmos by *sinful* first parents? Why did Jesus have to die for us, as well as for Adam and Eve, who committed the original sin in space and time? Why do we even have these 'first sinners' as our parents? Could we not have had 'first saints' as parents? Did we really need any parents at all in order to *be*, to be human *persons*, and to be joyful *with* God forever? Human persons do not *necessarily* need parents. Adam and Eve did not.

The Theology of Unconscious Denial?

If theologians stopped and really thought about it, they could not honestly claim that God works *interpersonally* in redeeming and saving us, but not in creating us. Nor could they say implicitly that God's gifting us to *be out of nothing* could have been an *impersonal* activity—such as breathing life into Adam—without there being an interpersonal exchange underlying it. That kind of creation would have to have been remedial, whereby God created Adam and his progeny out of *something*—out of something lame or crashed, not pristinely out of *nothing*.

God, for instance, does not have lungs. So, even if part of the *Genesis* story of creation *out of something* can be taken literally, the Scriptural *breathing* and *making* need to be understood figuratively or symbolically. God's creating us *out of nothing*, however, was at least as *inter*personal as Jesus was throughout his life among us—from his conception and birth to his crucifixion and resurrection.

Theologians are not likely to welcome the idea that each one of us was created out of nothing as a perfect finite person with perfect (finite) freedom and love. They have little basis for thinking, likewise, that at creation *out of nothing* we were *face to face with God's infinitely gifting freedom and love,* though not yet face to face with God's glory. And they might be inclined to suppress these ideas because of the startling implications about the slow growth in our understanding of Christian doctrine.

In any event, *Genesis* seems to be quite *impersonal* in the telling of creation. From dust, God fashions a body for Adam and starts to breathe into it a living soul. Adam is put to sleep while God fashions Eve from a rib. We might wonder, then, whether Adam and Eve said, "Thank you." And the text should leave us asking how in the world this event could have been human nature's *first introduction to the infinitely personal God of love.*

The *paradoxical* truth is that the creation *out of nothing* had to be *interpersonal,* both on God's part and on our part. Otherwise, we cannot really believe that God is *both* infinitely good *and* infinitely powerful. Only in the context of faith or belief that God's goodness and power are *infinite* can we see that God created us *perfect* in our being, *in our freedom,* and in our ability to love.

We ourselves must have faltered, then, in receiving our *being.* God did a perfect gifting to us by infinite goodness and infinite power. But we must have rendered ourselves immediately *impersonal.* By our *maybe* response, *we* failed to fulfill our perfect (finite) freedom-power. This power was not at all passive, but perfectly active: an ability to say fully *yes* to being who we are. Multitudes of *maybe*-sayers (persons who would become eventually-generated human persons in space and time—including Adam and Eve, the first to be rehabilitated through space and time) made themselves impersonal to one degree or another. In responding *maybe,* some could have said *yes* with greater or lesser strength than others. The intensity of the originatively-personal *maybe*-sayers likely varied.

Creation *out of nothing* must have been done all at once: for every *person*—human and angelic. There could have been no space-time aspect about it—no this *then* that. Rather, there had to be the unique interpersonal creation of each person at once, done effectively in one eternal moment. One might say, on "God's time," not ours. (Created persons are *from* this eternal moment, and they are *within* it; but they are not eternal. That is, we are not as God is: with no beginning and no end. We are immortal or "everlasting," so to say, but not eternal.)

No Temptation

Creation *out of nothing* had nothing imperfect about it, including temptation. No one tempted us. God created us with perfect freedom that was unhindered by temptability. God *could* not subject Adam or Eve or any of us to temptation at this absolutely first moment, and retain integrity as God.

Even a human creator tests "products" only because they might be weak. No need to test anything known to be perfect. But, at our first moment, we were perfectly strong in freedom and ability to love. By God's grace of creation, we were perfect in our freedom: our ability to determine entirely our own acts and our living forever. Our faulty response was *entirely our own will.*

Our pristine response to creation must have involved some kind of willingness to receive a being other than the one we were being given. We might have "tempted ourselves" by wanting a being that was infinite, like the being of God. We surely must have damaged our freedom severely by any willingness to entertain a reception of a different being than the one with which we were being gifted. Even a partial desire to have an infinite being, like that of the Ones gifting us, would have done incredible harm. It would have rendered us susceptible not only to tempting ourselves again, but to being tempted by others, notably the agents of Satan.

We made ourselves weak by our first, deficient act of receiving our being. We exercised our perfect freedom imperfectly. *We* did it; not our perfect power of freedom. Our *freedom* did not act. Our *act* did not act. *We* personally acted defectively, and abused our perfect exercise of freedom-power.

Perfect finite beings are something like Jesus, who is perfect as an infinite being. Even within the desert after the forty days of fasting, confronted by the evil one, Jesus was tortured, but not tempted. He could not sin, and so it was not real temptation on the part of Jesus, but only on the part of the self-deceiving Satan.

We *could* sin at the moment of creation out of nothing because we were *finite* beings, able to say *yes* or *no* fully on our own—with our perfect freedom. Since we said less than *fully yes*, we became quite temptable, as well as redeemable. Saying *fully yes* would have put us in heaven; saying *fully no* would have locked us in hell. Saying less than either *yes* or *no* has put us here in the precarious world of space and time. Destined for death and final judgment.

We must now be *repressing spiritually* this first act of our be-ing: our self-numbing act of responding to creation. Spiritual *repression*, the *unconscious denial* of what we know or suspect to be true, must be incredibly powerful. This unconscious denial of who God really is and who we are is much stronger than its well-known counterpart within us: the repression of unwanted *emotions* and of unpleasant *experiences* in earthly life.

In the 20th century, we became particularly well-acquainted with our common ability to repress selectively unwanted feelings and experiences. Such may be designated emotional repression. Most psychoanalysts have given much systematic attention to unconscious thoughts and desires. But until now we have hardly suspected the reality of *ontological* repression—repression of a part of our being, *by* that being itself. Yet this manner of repression—the repression of meanings and of dimensions of our being—must be ruling over all our other repressions. The spiritual governs the emotional.

Deeper Than Eden

Adam's headship of the human race, then, must have had an origin deeper than the actions of Eden. *When God said "Be,"* right out of nothing, we said, *"Maybe."* Adam and Eve did, likewise. A kind of *yes/no* response. That lack of a full *yes* response to our being—but not a complete *no* response—must have prompted God's willingness to attempt to save us from ourselves, and from our self-induced mediocrity that would have otherwise led us to ruin.

In the fullness of time, our personally original sin (an originative sin) eventually evoked the Savior of the world, who is Christ, our Lord. He became one of us in order to lead us, through life and death, to the *threshold of forever* and to receive our final, lasting response to *be-ing*: be it *fully yes*, or *fully no*. There is no possibility for *maybe* in heaven or in hell. We are headed either for a full *yes* or a full *no*. Christ is our personal Savior much deeper than we have believed consciously.

We have been taught, however—or at least we get the definite impression—that we were created out of nothing only at the moment of conception within our mothers. But that is to claim that creation *out of nothing* resulted in something imperfect. As beautiful as every mother's body is, there is nothing *perfect* about it or about resulting zygotes and embryos. Even the healthiest are flawed. Eventually, all will "die the death," before or after birth.

Creation out of *nothing* is not an event at *conception*. Thinking so, makes God subject to giving *being* at the prompting of sin—say, teenagers in the back seat of a car. Theology, then, would seem to be regarding God actually as willing to be a kind of partner in our sin—a kind of *deus ex machina*, a convenient cover for ignorance about originative beginnings.

On the contrary, the whole of the cosmos—all of space and time—would seem to be the self-induced, cosmic concentration camp, from which no one gets out alive. Super-blessedly, as Christians believe, God took on our mortal flesh and was born in the poverty of a stable. Jesus matured in wisdom and grace. Then he proclaimed the Good News of our redemption and possible salvation. Suffering horribly, he died, and rose from the dead to live and rule forever. By his Resurrection he set us free to *live*, in and through his grace and our Faith, a Renewed Freedom—a freedom to say *fully yes* to being-at-all and to being *who* we were, and still are, meant to *be*.

Chapter 2

The "Original Choice" of Adam and Eve

Adam and Eve stand under a tree eating a forbidden fruit. Both of them agreed to eat by taking advice from the serpentinian tempter.

Was the act of consuming the fruit an error? Some believers today think so. But the traditional view is that this infamous "first choice" was an act of defiance. Adam and Eve made more than a mistake. They were *willing* to do what God solemnly told them not to do. Their ill will made them sinners. They *deliberately* distorted what they knew, and hereby "missed the mark." Their sin had more than massive consequences for themselves and for all their offspring.

But what about us, their progeny? Were we *shoved off* the mark? In other words, did Adam and Eve "make us do it"? Was our inheritance of their disobedience an 'unfortunate circumstance'? Did we inherit quite innocently their offense or, at least, its sinful consequences? These questions and many others deserve our best response.

We can begin by reviewing briefly how Adam and Eve became established in this world of space and time.

Clues in *Genesis*

The *Book of Genesis* says that in the beginning, God created the heavens and the earth. This material world began to be by the infinite activity of One whose power is eternal. But the whole created world, including angelic and human persons, is finite, and not eternal.

Indeed, the kinds of things that were created in the world of matter show up in stages. They go from the simply physical, such as sand and rocks, to the complexly biological, such as plants and animals, to human persons, all by an upward moving hierarchy.

At first, we are informed that there was a "formless void." This picturesque manner of speaking in *Genesis* might mean to some that every element of the whole works *ultimately* came "out of nothing." Or, less metaphorically, it might more likely refer to the particular elements of the cosmos, such as light, air, water, plants, birds, and so forth—that were made from *something*: *ultimately* from a void, if not from chaos.

For instance, *Genesis* reports God's words, "Let there be light." But *how* light came to be is not said. We are told simply *by whose executive power* light came on the scene. Importantly, the author seems to be stating definitely that the various elements of space and time came into existence successively and in a certain order under some commanding power.

Creation "out of nothing" (*ex nihilo*), however, could not have been like this. It could not be a process. Creation out of nothing is immediately and fully effective. It is flawless. There is simply the full and perfect gift of unique created persons, given by an infinitely good Creator in this immediate way.

So, in *Genesis* we see a creation "out of something" (*ex aliquo*). Whether one's interpretation happens to be literal or figurative, God is said to make things gradually, step by step, as it were. Starting from a void, God forms day and night, the earth and stars, the plants and animals, and eventually a man and a woman.

As well as being the supreme Creator of the elements—*ultimately* from nothing—God is presented as a *maker* who uses pre-existing materials to form new creations. Adam was made from the dust of the earth, and Eve from a rib of Adam.

The basic creation of the material world was done in six "days," most likely meaning six lengths of time, *not necessarily* 24-hour periods. The coming of evening and morning during these days could readily be seen symbolically rather than literally. In any case, taken either literally or figuratively, these six days indicate a process and progression—whether or not the "leaps" from lower to higher forms were lightening fast or massively gradual.

So, on the seventh day, God "rested," possibly suggesting that it took effort, as it were, to craft the whole cosmos. Not that God had to fight hostile spirits, in the way that various pagan stories held, but that the matter of the stages of *this* creation had to be "worked" to conquer its passivity, its active resistance. (It was also a way of telling people to be God-like and to rest on the Sabbath day in their covenant with the Creator.)

Augustine, the classic Christian theologian, seems to have taken God's creating activity to be "immediate" and "simultaneous," and as occurring on "one day." He held, however, that some things were created whole and actual and that others were created as potential and destined to unfold gradually. So, even he saw original creation as involving some imperfection or lack of fulfillment and thus as involving a process.

Despite this special intuition about God and creation, Augustine still seems to miss the full force of the creation *ex nihilo and its utter immediacy.*

On the one hand, such creation could be *only* of *perfect* persons, effected by the infinitely perfect act of God. These created persons are not "gifted" with *any* passive potency (ability to be *done to*) or with any processes. They are perfect, purely actual, finite beings (with abilities to be and do).

On the other hand, *subpersonal* beings are necessarily *imperfect.* They were created out of some kind of a *void*—not out of "nothing." A "void" is basically an emptiness within something, perhaps within a fullness. What is the something, the fullness, for this void?

The whole cosmos and its effects could only have been caused by God working on what originatively perfect persons *produced* by *responding imperfectly* to their pristine creation.

Some have taken the *Genesis* story as reporting a vision that was communicated to Moses (or to Adam) about the origins of the world, and that it was not a report of physical events necessarily. However, the world that such vision would be *about* can now be seen directly. It is process-ridden and imperfect. Even if the "six days" are strictly methodological and pedagogical devices to make it easier to understand the world's origin, that world still thunders its deficiencies.

In any case, the main point of the two creation accounts in *Genesis* is that it sketches out God's masterful authority and command.

Genesis: the Impersonal Creation

When we examine the texts, despite particular discrepancies, we find that the relationship of creatures to the Creator is depicted as rather impersonal. Even the life breathed into Adam (in the "second" creation account) is being treated as less than fully personal. God "breathing" on the newly formed, not-yet-alive creature is hardly relating Person-to-person. This act is basically Person-to-thing.

Here we find a clue to something significant about the nature of the cosmic creation. This material creation is not person-centered, but function-centered. It is essentially a means to an end. Its purpose would appear to be a process of recovery. Certainly, the purpose of this material creation—with its *intrinsic passivity*—is *not simply* for the glory of being.

The making of Adam and Eve is characterized in rather functional terms. Adam comes from the dust of the earth and Eve from the rib of Adam. This activity seems to be continuous with the making of the impersonal forces and factors of the cosmos during the other five days of creation.

Whether the time is regarded as short or long—six days or sixteen billion years—both creationists and evolutionists treat creation as a *process*. The creation goes from stage to stage. All or most of the creatures are seen as coming out of something else—if only out of a void or chaos.

Such a creation is in no way "creation out of nothing" (*ex nihilo*), but "out of something"—out of something that is ready to "be done *to*" or acted *upon*. (God is not a Magician, pulling pure creatures out of, or through, imperfect ones. Or plopping perfect creatures out of nothing into the procession of imperfect ones.) This "creation" or *making* includes a space-time framework, even as does the account of Adam and Eve in Eden before the "fall."

From whatever angle we view it, there is nothing perfect about the creation of passive matter and motion. All things therein—in "the heavens and the earth"—though good, are not perfect. Despite their amazingly intricate structure and beauty, these things all have imperfections.

We read that God is pleased with the levels of this creation *ex aliquo* (out of something). Each is declared to be good. God even dialogues with God when determining to create man and woman in the divine likeness.

But, at the moment of the making, so to speak, God is not depicted in dialogue with those creatures themselves. God does not directly *speak with them*. There is no *immediate* "God said, we said." *This* creation has noticeably less than an *inter*personal effect.

In the second account (*Genesis* 2), the activity of God is portrayed as more personal than in the first account. God talks to Adam and tells him what is good and bad.

Yet, Adam and Eve in the Garden of Eden were not in heaven. Immediately, there was a question about what they should or should not do. Such a question could not have arisen in heaven, where there would be only supreme light, harmony, fulfillment, and peace.

Of the fruit of all the trees in the Garden, except one, they were permitted to eat. Adam and Eve had a continuing choice of doing good or doing bad. They were obviously living with God on a trial basis. An obviously imperfect way of living.

Their interpersonal relationship with God and with each other was not a union of rapturous bliss. They had the real, ongoing prospect of saying *no*, as well as *yes*. Although they seemed to be on good terms with God, Adam and Eve were far from being continuously and ecstatically intimate with the divine. Moreover, they were far from being at home with each other. They were conversant, but not contented.

Before they sinned, they were naked and unashamed. Quite naive.

Right after their fall, they were embarrassed to be in front of each other. They also hid from the presence of God, indicating perhaps that they had been unaware of how they looked before their sin.

Their hiding would seem to mean that they were not only ashamed of disobeying God, but also of how untrustworthy they had been in the Garden from the start. Their yielding easily to temptation should have revealed *to them* their initial naiveté about how lacking in intimacy of relationship they were with each other and with God, even *before* the sin.

The *functionality* of their bodies—naked or otherwise—meant that they were designed for work, more than for celebration. After they completely succumbed to the wishes of the tempter, unwanted self-knowledge was brought to light by their sin. They *experienced* both guilt and shame.

But there was a difference between their guilt and their shame.

Guilt involves the awareness of having done something wrong: remorse about disobedience. Shame, however, is much more than distress over having *acted* wrongly. Shame involves disgrace about being who one is: an unworthiness of be-*ing*, not just of be-*havior*.

Although they did not realize it at the time, Adam and Eve were *dis*-graced even before they made their wrong choice of *action*. And once they disobeyed God's command, their bad choice of behavior triggered their remorseful awareness of *what kind of being* they were: weak and temptable.

They alone could have *made themselves* that way: disgraceful while completely denying it even to themselves. Their original sin of *misbehavior* over the fruit of a tree made them confront their own ill will *and* their less than perfect condition of *being*.

The structure of their observable selves, with all their functional bodily parts, especially organs of social generation (their genitals), reveals them as needing recovery, individually and communally. Even before the explicit temptation from the evil one under a tree, they were living in a manner quite like the way they existed after the fall. They did not stand *in the Garden* as perfect created persons.

Why So Functional?

Why were they standing *there*? Why *in a garden*? And why did they require food at all? Why did they need a mouth and the whole complex of internal organs and cells that comprise their spatial and temporal manner of being as individuals?

Were they not created "a little less than the angels"? Not at all as angels, of course. But, at the moment God said *Be*, did they not encumber themselves by their response and load themselves with the weights of space and time, and of *passivity* in their matter?

Surely, Adam, Eve, and all other human persons could have been created as human persons, *but without any passivity in either their matter or their spirit*. Passivity necessarily signifies *the* condition of *imperfection*.

Their *originative* creation "out of nothing" could not possibly have involved *any passive* matter. There was simply *active matter* (pure receptivity of essence) proper to perfect *human* beings. There could have been no bodily—and hence ontologically imperfect—structure to their gifted beings.

Adam and Eve would receive, of course, functional bodies at the moment of their creation out of dust and out of a rib—out of some kind of passivity. (And we would likewise in space and time be created redemptively out of the widely fragmented condition of *our* originative be-ings.) This beginning "make over" of their self-afflicted beings was a necessary part of the prospects for *fallen* human beings to emerge from the repression and the denial of their *originative* response to creation.

Indeed, the portrayal of Adam and Eve as having been created from the dust of the earth and a rib shows their impersonal condition that was not directly *ex nihilo* (out of nothing). Thereupon, God was working with them in the process of the recovery from the crashed condition *ex nihilo* that had occurred "well before" the Garden experience of making an "original choice." (Original, that is, in space and time.)

Being bodily, with organs, necessarily signifies neediness, despite how well supported by conditions of pleasure and satisfaction. The specific reason for organs is to be a means to an end. While organs can be treated as ends in themselves momentarily by our attitudes, they are in themselves "fleshly tools" (etymologically stated)—the means to maintain a whole that is greater than themselves. That *whole* is ordered to redemption, far more than to creation.

Even the whole organismic body itself is essentially a means, not an end. The physical body—however "perfect" it might seem—is functioning in every cell for the good of something *other* than that cell itself. And so it was in Eden, even before the fall. Such is not the condition of perfection, even when the *functioning* is often seen to be "perfect functioning." Perfect *functioning* is not perfect *being*.

People usually think of the human body as a means the soul uses to know physical reality—specifically knowing *through* the senses. They rarely wonder, however, why the body would be required for the person to know physical things. Why not know physical things in a non-sensory way, something like God and the angels do?

Why not know all of cosmic reality, as a whole and in every part, through spiritual powers alone, in a manner similar—but not at all identical—to the way of the blessed angels? Did God just arbitrarily decree it to be that way, or is there some necessary reason for our functionality to be based in passivity? Death, of course, is a major result of functional passivity.

The sin of Adam and Eve—traditionally called original sin—could have been perhaps *an initial stage in arousing recognition*. This fault could have revealed to them that their spatiotemporal bodies were a sign of an already committed *originative sin*. Right from the start in the Garden, even before succumbing to the serpentine temptation, they might well have been called to recover from a *protoconscious* sin that was, at that point, spiritually unconscious (preconscious).

Their bodies were not evil at all. Their bodies were serving as *part* of the means for their *recovery*, and for the recovery of succeeding generations of fallen human persons—recovery from an *originative* sin. At the same time, their bodies, because destined for death, were serving as sacral signs that an originative sin had been done *by themselves* to their whole *being*. But the messenger (the body) should not be blamed for the message. Similarly, our bodies should not be regarded as bad news, just because they represent recovery from the originative bad news within us.

No *immediate* creature of God could have been imperfect, except by *self*-diminishment. Even before their sin with the serpent, Adam and Eve had bodies that consisted of "parts outside of parts." These parts were specifically *means* to the functioning of other parts and of the whole. Having "parts outside of parts" means distension, the condition of being not fully or perfectly integral. In a spatialized body, the integrity of being is inherently compromised. The whole of the physical body stands as redemptively good, but is not an originative condition of being for anyone.

In *Genesis* we find no specific expression of man and woman being created "out of nothing." How could there be? Such a creation would have been immediately *personal*, and could not have been anything as impersonal and as functionalistic as God blowing breath or constructing one body from part of another.

Creation *ex nihilo* is the *infinitely intimate* act of love that creates the *finite* power to be loving—interpersonally and unconditionally. This primal created power is intended immediately for *celebrational life everlasting*, not for functional temporal survival.

By contrast, the creation stories of *Genesis* are "process stories." They may have symbolic reference to creation *ex nihilo*. They serve mainly, however, as ways to account for the early stages of God's *redemptive and restorative* activity. By attempting to reform imperfect creatures into newness of being, God begins to reclaim, from self-diminishment, the immensely resistant "human race."

The whole of the Hebrew and Christian Scriptures seems directly concerned with *redemptive* creation—and not originative creation. This redemptive activity involves a whole mega-process of bringing to potential recovery—eventually in the Messiah—self-depressed created persons. The hopeful prospect emerges that, despite their precariously processive existence, these persons will become *willing* to be *awakened* and *receive* restoration. Restoration cannot be done merely *to* them (impersonally). It will have to be fully *received by* them (interpersonally).

The Big Implication

Some people take the *Genesis* story of creation literally; others, symbolically. However it is interpreted, the revelation seems open to the idea that we *deserved* to inherit the resultant original sin.

If we had not sinned originatively, how could we be in the present predicament? An infinitely good, infinitely powerful, and infinitely creative God would have given us innocent parents, not guilty ones. Rather, there would be no need for parents at all, much less a line of parentage. So, realizing that *God's "integrity" is infinite*, we can also be sure that we deserve our present inheritance.

Suppose we were to take the Eden story rather figuratively—at its "root" level. Then it could mean that Adam and Eve had a deeper choice than eating or not eating the fruit of a tree. It could mean symbolically, yet quite really, that they had the choice whether to receive well, or not so well, the gift of being. According to such an interpretation, Adam and Eve, responding to the gift of being-at-all, apparently had some kind of a problem with saying fully "yes."

In this illustrative way of looking at the story, the prime couple had full personhood before God. But they *freely* desired to be the supreme source of their own life. They stumbled over the prospect of being merely finite.

In other words, they fell into making a root-level *contrast*. They compared themselves with *God*. God, however, is entirely beyond *comparison*. Their depth-response was hardly the unconditionally loving gratitude that the gift of being—gifted from the heart of God directly—should evoke, spontaneously, freely, and intimately.

They did not respond generously to their Creator. Instead, it would seem they turned one eye (figuratively speaking) toward themselves. They *freely* diverted themselves away from God. Therefore, we might say that the infinite "difference" (not distance) between their own being and the being of God, actively bringing them to *be*, could have *occasioned* their unwillingness.

This "infinite difference" in *kind* of being could *not* have *caused* their hesitation about being who they were gifted to be. Their reluctance to *be* the being God gave them was undertaken freely. But such a difference between themselves and God would have been their freely chosen *excuse* for their freely faltering receptivity.

At the moment God willed them to be and to be themselves, they must have balked. As God gave them their whole and perfect finite being, they received it freely by partially denying who they were being gifted to be. They *did not fully* affirm their being-with God and thereby enter heaven. Neither did they fully say *no* and create a hellish destiny.

To the very act of God, they answered in a less than perfect way. They did so *by the gifted, perfect power of freedom itself.* They must have said, in effect, both *yes* and *no* to the sheer *gift* of being-at-all.

As a result, they became virtually powerless to be who they were. Yet they had *not fully* rejected God and their own being. So, in the divine goodness and mercy, God was able to revive them. This "re-creation" started to occur right from within their already existing, self-decimated being. And *that* creation—creation *ex aliquo* ("out of something")—is taken up by the accounts in the *Book of Genesis*.

The creation stories in *Genesis* then are versions of the beginning of our *remedial or redemptive* creation. Such activity of God is not the creation of the whole being of each person "out of nothing." It is the making of a new and functional *part* of him or her. This newly developed *part* of a crashed creature comprises the functional, soul-body existence within space and time, that is attained at the moment of conception; it serves as a kind of ontological placenta or service organ of the originatively created person.

This serviceable manner of existence in which we are now living is designed to assist in the awakening of the whole person to his or her comatose, crashed condition of being. We failing persons now exist in the self-inflicted darkness that was caused by our originative decision. We need awareness of origins and of the magnitude of our alienation from God.

As one of the Scriptural accounts indicates, the world of matter was gradually formed, "day by day," until it was made ready for the entry of Adam and Eve *as existents in space and time*. According to the new perspective, however, at that point they had already sinned *originatively*.

Their personal *originative* sins *and ours* had created chaos in our being. The creation stories of *Genesis* start from this condition. The first couple was created *ex aliquo*—out of a chaotic state of being.

Only after their original sin in Eden could they and their offspring eventually, or even possibly, come to understanding *why* they were functionally made in Eden and why they were to be banished.

The grossly impersonal cosmos is an orderly formation of passive matter and motion. This "cosmess" of good and evil is something that *we* caused, *not to be*, but to *ex*-ist. This kind of be-ing stands outside itself, is somewhat alien to itself, and "begs" to "return" to the "freedom of the children of God."

The original choice of Adam and Eve, evoked in the Garden, made it *possible* for the coming of much deeper awareness—an awareness of the *being*-based character of our sin and of God's infinitely loving response that includes our redemption and the *opportunity* for our salvation.

Chapter 3

The Fallen Freedom of Adam and Eve

The original choice of Adam and Eve in the Garden of Eden was a symptom-sin. It was the first of the symptoms of the originative sin committed by all of us earth-dwellers at the moment that we were created all at once, "before" space and time began.

By responding with hesitation to the gift of being, we violated the perfect freedom of our being and crashed into the condition of passivity. We created a big bang of explosive energy that radiated outward in order to form the physical universe. Today this radiation is known as *energy*, which means the capacity to do work. But, in the absolute framework of being, it could be considered as the capacity to do the work of recovery from our personal 'fall from being.'

Together, all of those who immediately said *maybe* "contributed" collectively to the whole field of cosmic energy. Their 'half-hearted' responses to the gift of their being caused a tremendous reaction that became an evolving energy toward recovery.

The *Book of Genesis* begins with an account of how God created us—that is, restored us as planetary human beings—redemptively, *ex aliquo* (*out of something*: darkness, chaos, dust, a rib, or, in the term of our times, energy). The explosion of our original being, caused by our maybe-attitude produced the existence of passive-reactive energy—part of the power to do the work needed to restore self-damaged persons. The incarnate Christ drew upon this energy in redeeming the fallen human community.

Adam was created from this energy as the first in the line of fallen humans. Eve was then created from the same source, that is, from cosmic energy, but through Adam's "rib." And the remainder of fallen humankind followed.

When Adam and Eve were created out of the elements of Eden, they showed how naïve they were about their condition. They were not ashamed of being naked or of having a pleasant life eating the fruits and cultivating the earth around them. They were unaware of how shameful it was to be persons who were not in perfect union with God, who had gifted them with personhood—directly like the divine—and whom they had been called to worship and to be-with forever *immediately*. They did, of course, have a companionship with God in the Garden, but far from an absolutely free and ecstatic friendship.

Immediately after their disobedience in the Garden they noticed that they were naked. We are inclined to think that it was their sin, right then and there, that caused their nakedness to be shameful. Fixed on the linear, horizontal meaning of the text, we are unaware of the vertical meaning: that even to have bodies from dust or a rib and to have an immediate environment of impersonal nature reveals that a great fall had already transpired in their *be*-ing.

Adam and Eve had been cast out before they showed up in Eden. And we all seem to be cast out about *being* "cast out." As their followers, we tend to do one or another of two opposites. Either we blame matter as being bad and something to be ashamed of or we praise matter as a way of being that God chose for us by original intention. We unconsciously deny the intrinsic deprivation of being that all passivity in matter necessarily represents.

Matter Is Good and Healing

Passive matter is a *sign* that grave sin has been committed. But it is not matter that is bad. Matter is good and redemptively needed to bring us back from our originative *maybe*-response to *be*-ing. Matter is not to be blamed nor is it anything to be ashamed of. We who must live an earthly life—a purgative life—should be ashamed of our sin—the originative response we gave to our be-ing. That purely spiritual act of *maybe*-saying caused the need for the "energy of redemption" including the whole world of space and time.

Attributing to matter our self-numbed condition of spiritual being is like blaming the crutches of a crippled person for the impairment. We cannot take away the infirmity by taking away its remedies. Misconstruing the text of *Genesis* on the prime origin of our shame, we overlook the prime reason for it. Adam and Eve should have been ashamed that they had to be revived by way of dust and a rib in the midst of impersonal nature, including a serpent slinking around a tree ready to strike doubt in their minds about the truthfulness of God. Instead, they became shamed only upon their disobedience to God's command about eating a forbidden fruit. That sin was their first sin in space and time, but not first in be-ing. Their original sin of history confirmed their originative sin in be-ing

We all inherited Adam's sin. But *in that* sin is contained all of the personal (originative) sins of those who responded *maybe* to God's absolute, *interpersonal*, creation *ex nihilo* (*out of nothing*).

Adam and Eve also responded *maybe*. They were chosen as the first crashed humans to be rehabilitated. So, they bore the weight of the sins of all *being-hesitaters*, including their own. Our first parents started us on our struggle through space and time: a purgatory for *maybe*-sayers to "get their *act* together."

This earthly life provides some beginning stability for all of us, in order that we can start to wake up. We need to realize what *God* did in creating us perfect out of nothing, what *we* did to ourselves by our response, and to know *why* we are here and not fully united with our Creator at this very moment.

Before the fall, Adam and Eve were naïve—*not innocent*—about their nakedness. They should have been appalled that there was dust, energy, and passive matter all around them. Why not find brilliant spiritual light and full intimacy with their Creator?

But their shame should not have been about having bodies or the about the matter itself. Rather, about what matter and even energy manifests. The whole world of the Garden of Eden, with all of its material magnificence, should be a blatant manifestation about their and our unwillingness to be perfectly as God gifted us—without any need for matter.

Even before Eve came on the scene, God warned Adam not to eat of the fruit of a certain tree in the Garden, by saying, "The day you eat of it, you shall die the death." (*Gen.* 2:16) God did not sound confident that Adam was reliable even then. The words sound like a foregone conclusion. That is because Adam had already sinned and was decisively weakened by it. By being given a body, he was being brought back from disaster. Matter and body are necessarily passive, and basically so. They originate from passive-reactive energy, the inherently redemptive effect of the crash of our originatively fallen freedom.

We are in this world of living and dying in order to come to know, love, and serve our Creator and Redeemer. In that way, we prepare ourselves for entry into full communion with one another within the infinitely loving heart of God. By divine Love, we came to *be*, and by that Love we are now be-*coming*—coming back to be-*ing*, if we are finally *will*-ing.

Each one of us receives our body, formed within our self-deprived being. By means of our parents' act of generation, God begins our redemption. Our body is completely and naturally subjected to our fallen condition of *passivized* receptivity (called passive potency). Likewise, our soul and its spiritual powers of intellect and will are permeated by *spiritual* passive potency. This bodily creation out of something, spoken about in the first words of *Genesis*, is not at all the same as the creation out of nothing.

But this creation of material being is *all good*. Many religionists and philosophers over the ages have treated matter as evil or as a drag on our existence. But matter is necessary for the redemptive recovery of our originative being. Though cosmic energy is a result of a fall in be-ing and comes from the *no* in our *maybe*, it is a critically needed good for reparation. In our tradition, by regarding matter as somehow bad, many seem to have "shot the messenger." Energy is an imperfect power. We need *infinitely perfect power*— divine power—to work gracefully with the passivity in our human condition.

The Two Creations Interacting Together

Redemptive creation and originative creation could not possibly be the same. *Out of nothing*, God could create *only* perfect persons. God could not be *God* and create *anyone* imperfect. Because of even the slightest unwillingness from us to be whom we were gifted to be, the very first creation resulted in the need for "the redemption of many."

The whole cosmos—all passive-reactive matter and motion—is manifestly imperfect in being. Even in Eden, Adam was not a perfect person. He was lonely and looking for a companion among the animals. The present world, then, comes *redemptively* from the hand of God, who "works" with it to restore all things in Christ Jesus. But it comes *primarily* from *us*, originative sinners, who are "naturally resisting" the salvific work of God. We resist because of the self-twist we gave our nature at the moment we were created out of nothing.

In the future, theology needs to make better attempts to help us deepen our roots, and thereby to *receive* sacred Revelation with *ever deeper* understanding and love. Then we can enjoy the perfect being that we still *are, as gifted forever*, while we are also repenting for our personal originative sin that made us also imperfect beings for now—if not forever.

We need to realize that the revelation of our having committed an originative sin is a discovery that we must do for ourselves. God lets us come to the realization on our own. God's infinite freedom allows us to realize this truth in our own way. And if, in this life, we do not come to know consciously our personally originative sin, we will be directly confronted with it at the moment of death. At that point, those who are humble will acknowledge; the proud and rebellious will adamantly refuse.

Tragically, the theological tradition has been drawn too heavily into Augustine's thought on the *inheritance* of what has been called original sin. This seminal theologian and dramatic convert to Christianity had been fearful of returning to his Manichean, gnostic or elitist ideas about our origins. He seemed to think that Adam must have been the first sinner, otherwise the idea of sin's origin would be an instance of a purely spiritual activity. But that would seem to make it necessary to believe in some kind of separation of the spiritual soul from the body even before the moment of conception within our mothers. So he had to blame Adam for the start of it *all*: the *only* start for us humans, according to his ruminations about it. From that perspective, we appear to be trapped in time, by and with Adam. Thus, there would be no pre-temporal way to account for our condition in being.

Instead, Augustine and the tradition could have realized that, in the Garden of Eden, Adam was alone *and also lonely*. A sure sign that sin had already occurred. The loneliness had to be caused by sin, not by God. So, even before the temptation and the "fall," Adam and Eve were already living out the beginning of their and our potential recovery from the sin that had occurred "before" space, time, and physical bodies began. Their eventual temptation and fall confirmed to them and to us how weak they were even before their appearance in an earthly Eden. (The word "before" is not used as a precedence in time, but in being.)

Augustine accepted the announcement by St. Paul that *in* Adam all have sinned. But he stopped there. He did not realize that if, *in* Adam, all have sinned, we must have sinned also *with* Adam. We sinned at the instant (non-durational, common moment) of creation out of nothing: the creation of persons only, the angelic and the human—a creation total and immediate. So, Augustine and the developing tradition have failed to recognize the deep *roots* of original sin: our personally *originative* sins. He could not see that each one of us has indeed inherited his or her own originative sin *in and through the inheritance* of the historical sin of Adam and Eve.

How We Are Perfect Beings Forever

We are greatly imperfect *as received by ourselves so far*. We received ourselves poorly at the originative moment of creation. And in our efforts every day, we can try to do better. By grace, we are called to be*come*: to lead redemptive lives of well-received suffering amidst joy, and to yearn—consciously, as well as unconsciously—for salvation by the *power* of God's incarnate Word.

We are, then, created persons who are *both* perfect *and* imperfect. Perfect forever because God's gift of being *as gifted* is inviolable and will last forever—whether in heaven or in hell. God is an infinitely perfect Gifter. When God says, 'Be and be perfect,' we *are* perfect *forever*. But we are imperfect now as *received* by us who immediately responded *maybe*.

God does not simply "give" us our being. There is no "handing over" something. We can know the difference between giving as a delivering or a 'handing over' something to someone and giving as gift-giving or gifting someone with grace and with the generosity of superabundance. Being is a sheer gift.

So, in the grace of creation, the gift of our being is perfect now, but *also* imperfect. And we will become grossly imperfect forever, if we finally fail to repent sincerely within the depths of our hearts for every personal sin, originative and derivative.

If we fail to receive salvation by Jesus Christ—at least, receive it implicitly or subconsciously in this world, and consciously in the moment of judgment at the time of death—the dark-side of our imperfectly received being will be set *forever to rebel* against our perfectly-gifted-side. This unimaginable conflict within our being will be a prime circumstance of everlasting self-punishment—along with the *everlasting* loss of union with God.

We must wholeheartedly repent, eventually and especially, for our first, irresponsible reception of the gift of our being—our flawed or "maculate reception." Let us hope and pray that many of us are even now repenting, at least unconsciously.

Christians believe that Baptism removes the condition of living in original sin, while still leaving us with the consequences that are called concupiscence. But they could become eventually aware that this sacramental removal also includes the *roots* of original sin. Baptism must take away our supremely personal *originative* sin, committed at the moment of being created out of nothing. This most personal sin helps to form, with all of the others, the roots of the original sin that, in the history of redemption, is called the sin of Adam. Without his originative sin, Adam would have immediately entered heaven, and we would have had to have a different personal progenitor on behalf of our redemption.

In any case, when we are judged at death, every planetary human being will be confronted by his or her originative sin, as well as by earthly sin. We need to be *really* willing, if not yet able consciously, to acknowledge our Creator's *immediately perfect and everlasting* gift of being. And we need to admit *our completely free, imperfect reception of be*-ing—of God's being as *Other*, and of our own being as *ours*. Our 'secret blaming of God' must stop in order that we may become the sons and daughters of an everlastingly joyous destiny: total union with the infinite goodness and glory of God.

Chapter 4

Actively Welcoming Our Being

We hold in our hearts our own being. Each person is gifted with an opportunity, not only about what to *do* today or tomorrow, but who he or she is going to *be* forever.

Our biggest situation in life, at every moment, brings on the pivot-question of how to treat our life itself. Will we ever welcome our being as an utterly incomparable gift? Will we thank the Gifter? Will we let ourselves be the person we were gifted to be or will we reject our life itself—and our very be-ing?

We can become a bit like the young fellow with his companions playing in the yard. He saw, across the street, an elderly man who was raking leaves. The man was known in the neighborhood for his thoughtfulness and kindness. The youngster said to his playmates, "Let's test the old guy's smarts. I just caught this bird. I'll put it behind my back and ask him to say whether the bird is dead or alive. If he says dead, I'll let it go flying. If he says alive, I'll crush it and hand it to him dead."

So, the little gang went smugly to the other side of the street and the prankster presented the man with the Big Question, "Sir, is the bird in my hand dead or alive?" The man paused for awhile, and then replied. "Son, the answer lies in your hands."

The answer to our everlasting destiny lies in our hearts—at the depths of our minds and wills. Not on the surface. God created us with perfect power to do our own living and being. And between our being and God's being is the radiation of relating as being with Being: God's grace.

But who will we be forever? *We* are now deciding—not God. We have already severely damaged our being by responding to the gift, at first, only partially. So, we are living here and now in order to stop the desire to crush "the bird in our hand": that is, to stop trying to possess the heart of our being. We are called to let ourselves become free from the depths of our selfishness by repenting for our failure to say *fully yes* to the *gift* of our being.

God created us by love *unlimited*. Therefore, we are *able* to know, even now, what *really* happened to us at the moment of creation. At that first instant, our pristine *attitude* was less-than-fully-positive about being-at-all and about being who-we-are. But we remain free to *redo* it, to change our fundamental attitude. At every present moment, it is really *possible* to say *fully yes* in profound gratitude for our being and for the hope that is within us.

One obstacle to doing so, however, is that we think God is really *all*-good and *all*-powerful. But this is not God. Indeed, there is no "all" about God. God is not limited by being a *whole* kind of being. In a whole being, there can be a 'filling up.' When we say *all*, for instance, we mean *every* bit. But there are no bits to God.

God is not a whole being. God is the infinite or *unlimited* kind of being. God's "wholeness" or integrity is unlimited. Calling God *all*-good or *all*-powerful demeans Yahweh or the Persons of divinity. And yet, here we are, doing it regularly in many of our thoughts, prayers, and preachings.

Nor should we mean that God has all the real good and all the real power. By *God's* doing, we who are created persons were gifted with, and received, our *very own* finite, *but real*, power and goodness. We did *not* receive *divine* power and goodness. Nor any *part* of it. God's freedom, goodness, and power are not finite. Our freedom, goodness, and power are all finite. These are real *gifts* to us and do not belong to God, thanks to God. They are not a loan; they are our own.

The Moment of Creation

At the moment of our absolute creation *out of nothing*, Yahweh or God—three infinitely powerful Persons—was the *only* Gifter of *being*. God's *infinitely* active ability created every person: each angel and each human. Every created person had *finite, purely active* potency—the power to *do* and to *be*, perfectly and finitely, whoever he or she had been gifted to be. God was present to us in infinite goodness and power, though not in glory. (The glory of God would come only to those who said completely *yes*—immediately or eventually.)

Originally, we were simply *receivers*—finite, but giftedly perfect. Each one was *perfectly free* to give a *fully grateful* response to the gift of being-at-all. By our first response, our very first act of *be*-ing, we were *able* to *be-with* God forever *immediately*. But *we who said 'maybe' received our being imperfectly*, and disabled it.

At that first moment of being, we were *empowered* to *be* and *do* only good. But we were also *able* to *do* our gifted be-ing as we *willed* to do. (Yes, it was our own and not a loan.) We willed to be something other than we were gifted to be. That act of our powers to know and love ravaged our being. Our freedom and ability to love were devastated.

This pristine calamity caused our present conditions of dullness in mind and heart. And it also caused the "crater" of our enormous unconsciousness, of which we are at present only darkly aware. With the "full authority of our perfectly-gifted being," we *passivized* ourselves. We caused our purely active potency to be-*come* passive.

At the moment of gifted being, we faced God with our purely active potency: the sheer ability to *do*. There was no created *passive* potency—no ability to *be done to* or *done in.* We actually caused our passivity instantly by the collapse of our being. So, we are now being called to recover, in all we do and think, from this passive potency of being "done to" or "done in" by ourselves and by others.

By our *maybe*-response, we had also caused (or "created") what we now call *energy*—the 'ability to do the work' of striving toward awareness of "what happened." The *partial yes*, within our *maybe*-saying, creates hope.

As we were being created out of nothing, we failed to *be fully ourselves*. We did so along with Adam, Eve, and multitudes of persons, both humans and angels. Perhaps eons of time transpired, along with the whirl of indefinitely gigantic galaxies of space. Nonetheless, within the forces of virulently-resisting, unconscious, broken human freedom, God was working with the ever-so-gradual, preparatory, subpersonal creation, the one that is *ex aliquo* (out of something)—the creation that, even now, comes out of *energy*: including space, time, matter, motion, plants, animals, and the rest.

God thereby created for *human* persons this beautiful planetary existence and rehabilitative center, known as earth. God *saw that it was good*. Not perfect. But quite capable of helping human persons begin to recover and to be restored.

Adam and Eve recovered from the crash by being restored out of their own fallen freedom, symbolized by the dust and the rib noted in *Genesis*. Similarly, within our mothers, we eventually began our recovery from this pristine fall. Out of the messy effects of our own personally fallen freedom, we began, at conception, our personal recovery—our be-*coming,* our being coming back to our original be-*ing*.

Creation and the Crash

At our creation out of nothing, divine goodness and power were *infinitely with* us—infinitely ready to receive us into everlasting life. We simply had to be fully willing to be exactly who we were. We know that multitudes of angels said *fully yes*. Perhaps, many human persons did also. Such persons would be bodiless, but would not be angels; just angel-like. (In *Psalms* 8:5 (8:6), God is said to create humans a little less than the angels. Perfect in their nature, but a lesser kind of nature.) Perhaps some, or many, humans said *fully no*, as did multitudes of angels, now known as devils.

Within God's *infinitely intimate* presence we were gifted to be ourselves *immediately and freely*. But, without any "assistance," we failed to receive fully this gift at that instant. We could have entered freely into heavenly union with the divine presence. Yet we did not act fully. We failed to give total thanksgiving for the gift of *being* and for the incomparable opportunity to be-*with* God, immediately forever.

This primordial "plunge" must have been personally, completely ours. God was the only Creator within the first and perfect creation. We had no potential tempter. At this instant of being created out of nothing, our tragic response was immediately and freely present.

Satan came to *be* at the same moment as we. He was completely involved in saying fully *no* ("I will not serve"). He must have begun his temptation-career "later," working on us who had created our own weakness and temptability by saying *maybe*. Chosen to be the initiators of the long line of humans in need of rehabilitation, Adam and Eve were the first to experience historically Satan's cunning ways of deception.

In responding *maybe*, we *"empowered"* ourselves to be *able* to choose evil...and we did! At one and the same moment out of nothing (*ex nihilo*), Adam and Eve, *together with us and multitudes of other perfectly created persons,* fell from their finite pure act of being into dark passivity. Is it any wonder that, after such a sin, they would resent themselves? Consciously or unconsciously.

The Creation of Space and Time

Immediately, with infinite love and patience, God began to work with our *maybe*-condition and with the chaos in which we left ourselves. Space-and-time itself was brought to exist by our *maybe*-saying. From the "cosmess," the Creator instantly began *developing* a cosmos, so that we humans could recover. So, here we are, "all spaced out, doing time."

In Eden, God began to "work" with Adam and Eve, who were chosen to be the first in line to be 'brought back.' Initiated by our *yes-no* hesitation in the beginning, we, as they, have been variously resisting recovery. In earthly life, God works—with infinite power upon simply finite, but resistant human *freedom*—to transform each of us. This work has been prepared for, over the ages, by God's fashioning of various kinds of imperfect creatures: from sub-atomics to atoms, from inorganics to organisms, from plants to animals.

We need to realize that God is infinitely powerful *for* us and *with* us, but not *over* us. God's power always works *with* us, never violating the freedom of created persons. Rather, we are offered the unlimited grace of encouragement in order that we can cooperate with Christ's redemption and finally be saved.

It does not matter whether this *ex aliquo* (out of something) kind of creation had occurred over several days or many eons. It was a *process*: a creation that was *not* out of nothing, but out of the passive-reactive energy that had resulted. Energy was the effect of the explosion caused by the massive crash of fallen human freedom at the instant of creation out of nothing.

Genesis reports—most likely figuratively—that a darkness and a chaos prevailed at or near the beginning of this creation (*ex aliquo*) out of something. The darkness and chaos did not come from God. Such was the result of our failed response to the gift of our being.

The earliest of God's work of recovery was started immediately upon our first faltering. Multitudes of suborganismic and organismic creatures gradually emerged. With the entry of Adam, from the dust of Eden, human history began. Then came Eve from the rib of Adam. All stages of creational development were the results of the divinely merciful, *instant response to our first failure*: falling into *maybe*, instead of responding straightforwardly *yes*.

Space and time began at the same instant as our *maybe*-response to creation *ex nihilo*. Space is the structural, physical result of our yes/no response. And time is the measure of meaning in motion.

Whether it took six calendar days or immense periods of time *via* evolution of some sort, the "work" was a process. It did not occur immediately, or all at once, as did creation *ex nihilo* (out of nothing). Passive potency (the condition of being "able to be done *to*") was involved. The collapse of our being was an *ontological (beingful) disorder*, done by abusing our pristine *freedom to be our being*. By this failure at the moment of creation, we have caused our gift to *be passivized*. We crippled our purely active power to *do*, and to *be forever with God*.

In effect, at our *conception* within our mother, we were gifted with the *placenta*-of-our-being: our body. And thereby we were rooted in the womb of space and time: the gracious, but defective, result of our fallen freedom.

All spatiotemporal matter is the result of *crushed, fragmented human freedom*. Every particle of matter of any kind—whether gas, liquid, solid, plasma, or whatever—could only have come from something imperfect and passivized, accompanied by a tremendous reaction in being itself. By the *no* within our *maybe* (*yes-no*), we exploded our being. But by the *yes* within our *maybe*, we remained redeemable.

God worked within our fragmented being and, over the vast stages of space and time, each of us eventually became conceived within our mother to begin our recovery. After the profound, ages-long, comatose condition of being, we began to return to originatively-gifted being. (This process did not involve re-incarnation. The notion of any kind of re-incarnation demeans the integrity of the body within the process of redemption. We have had no "previous existence" in this world of space and time. Before being conceived in our mothers, our fallen being must have existed in a 'pre-cosmos limbo.')

The vast process that is involved—whether evolutionary or not—is a critical part of God's *redemptive* creation. This divine endeavor is the process-creation or the *making* of new kinds of reality out of *something*—out of the huge explosion of energy that was a reaction to what we freely did to our perfect gift of being. *Genesis* has indicated the beginning of this process-creation by a void, darkness, dust, and such.

Passive matter did not come from or by God. God creates *directly and immediately* only perfect (finite) beings: persons with perfect freedom. There is nothing partial or imperfect about God's gift of our *being*. But by *receiving* the gift *imperfectly* we fractured our active-potency-to-be-who-we-are, and so the structure of this purely active potency exploded into passive potencies. We had abused thereby our own *personal* freedom, the only kind of being and freedom that God as infinite *could* have gifted: *perfect* finite being and perfect freedom.

Our matter and our bodily being did not come from angels. Those simply spiritual beings do not involve *matter* of any kind, including even the active matter (active receptivity in essence) with which we were originatively gifted. The only foundation for what we know as cosmic matter had to result from a crash in something finite that originally was in perfect freedom to remain perfect, but failed.

The fall from active to passive, resulted in a disaster that was tragic, yet redemptive. The reaction was partly redemptive because free created persons were hesitant, instead of fully negative. As a result, they could be revived. But their restoration has involved ages of time and small beginnings through the incomparably numerous types of matter and motion and an exquisite array of species that are found in the universe.

Even within the passivized matter we call the cosmos, and its largely dysfunctional fragmented elements, there is a big telltale indicator of our originative human freedom. Anyone can observe what philosophers have called *teleology*: the innate tendency of all cosmic entities—every body and particle—to act toward a specific end or purpose. Peach trees never produce apples or pine needles. They tend only to produce peaches. The laws of nature presume the predictable movements of matter. Even though these tendencies are not known in their details, they are banked on in every scientific endeavor. From the law of gravity to the indeterminacies of particles and waves, everyone presumes the basic stability of nature and its tendencies underlying all phenomena.

Our first freedom was completely spiritual. But every teleologic tendency in this fallen world represents the fall (or "plunge") from our originally perfect freedom, now trying to recover from *maybe*. Recovery could not be immediate, but only via the deep passivity of space and slow-movement in time. *Originative* sin has caused what might be called the "Big Bang of being." Space and time came to be, at that moment, by real human agents who defiantly exercised their perfect freedom at the moment of first creation.

Welcoming Redemption and Salvation

Christians believe that everyone was redeemed by Jesus Christ. But not that they are necessarily saved. Jews and others believe in the Messiah who will come and save his people. At least, we can agree that we all hold our own being in our hearts. All believers in God are challenged to receive *actively—not passively—*their own beings. Passive acceptance will not do. The opportunity at death is not about what to *do* today or tomorrow. We will necessarily decide: "Who am I going to *be* forever?"

So, it all comes down to the question of what we will say at death. Will we give our responses, as we did when we were gifted initially with our perfect being? God had said "Be, and be with Us," but we said *maybe.* Not with lips, but with our whole being. So, now we need to receive salvation not as we did with creation, but with a renewed spirit of being, yielding to the grace of full unity with God.

Our destiny lies in our hearts. Not in our mental or emotional heartfelt inclinations, but in the depths of our being. Who do we *will* to *be* and *with whom* do we *will* to be...forever? It has little to do with what we want, but with what we are *willing* to endure to arrive at God's will for us. Are we fully welcoming to our being and to the Being of God, who gifts us?

Chapter 5

Why Bad Things Happen to Good People

We do not believe deeply enough that we are incomparable gifts of God—to ourselves and to every other person. Consciously, and especially unconsciously, we are driven to wonder, "Why me?" We then see multitudes of others suffering obvious injustice and we wonder, "Why they?"

"Why do bad things happen to *innocent* people?" From the earliest times, this poignant question has been haunting Jews, Christians, and others. A contemporary poet, Les Murray, has said that, if people knew he (the author) had the answer to that question, they would shrink in terror.

We all know much more than we think we know. That is where the terror comes from. Unconsciously, for instance, we might even dare to suppose, with Karen Armstrong, a famous commentator on theology, who said that "if God could have stopped the proceedings at Auschwitz, but did not, he is a monster." We could be harboring that thought, unconsciously.

The existence of evil is a "mystery." That is the response of many theologians and philosophers of religion. True. But "mystery" can also be affirmed of chlorophyll, gravity, electricity, love, freedom, and countless other subjects right up to, and including, Christian teachings on the Incarnation and the Trinity. As Jacques Maritain, Josef Pieper, and many others have pointed out, a mystery is not an enigma or a puzzle, but a super-intelligible truth. Like fruit that is super-delectable, every mystery is super-intellectable. The meaning is inexhaustibly knowable to us.

Some pious people, however, have even counseled us to stop searching into the mystery of evil: that perhaps God has hidden the meaning of evil for our own good. That idea is unreasonable and virtually cynical. Jesus told his disciples that there were many things that they could not 'bear now,' but that the Spirit would teach in due time. (*John* 16:12-13) God intends us to know, to the best of our ability, everything that we can that is true, good, and meaningful: the better to love. Knowing more is for the sake of *loving* more.

Our Problematic Inheritance from Adam and Eve

The question *why* we inherited the sin of Adam and Eve, is rarely raised, let alone answered adequately. For many, the sin of Adam has amounted to an excuse, not a reason. But, if we participate ever more deeply in the mystery, we can begin to discover a reasonable response. We can come to *know consciously why* bad things happen to *all* people.

The "wings of Faith and Reason" must be strengthened, if we are going to address the mystery of evil, along with the mysteries of Redemption, Salvation, and *especially* Creation. St. John Paul II must have had our weakness in mind. He called for the philosophers of *being* to develop their reasoning. He expressed a desire that Faith be heightened and that we move beyond "the sterile repetition of antiquated formulae." He called for a dynamic philosophy of *being*, "based upon the very act of being itself." (*Fides et Ratio*, n. 97, 1998)

In other words, we need to develop our in-depth way of knowing events and spiritual meanings. We need to see not only 'a little way down,' but much deeper. For instance, Christians can contemplate Jesus on the Cross feeling abandoned on Good Friday, or they can mull over the sorrow of their Savior's knowing that multitudes will reject his sacrificial love. But these awesome concerns merely touch the issue of *why innocent* people suffer in the presence of God who is called, according to a traditional expression, 'all-good and all-powerful.'

The question is *not*: Why do many "innocents" apparently suffer far more than some people who are committed to evil? The question is: *Why* do the tiniest children suffer *at all*?

If we choose to join the blame chain by going back to the original sin of *Adam*, we are not going deep enough. We are simply missing the significance of this critical question: Why must anyone who is innocent suffer at all—anywhere along the line?

God Is More Than All-good and All-powerful

Nothing will move until we understand something typical about ourselves. We have been short-circuiting our knowledge of God by thinking and saying "God is all-good and all-powerful." Instead, we should be thinking and saying God is *infinitely* good and *infinitely* powerful.

There is no "all" to God. God is not "filled to the brim." Nor is God some purely *actualized* potency. God is not simply pure act. God is pure *infinite* act, and not pure finite act. We might often *say* that God is *infinite*. But do we really mean it? Or are we thinking of God unconsciously, but really, as merely an 'all-mighty Magician'?

The history of religious philosophy contains a grave impairment. We have confused an *infinitely* pure act of being (God) with what could be called a finitely pure act of being (a created person). All created beings, however, have been thought to be less than pure act. Even angels are regarded by our tradition as containing passive potency—at least, with respect to their essence. Passive potency is the condition of *being able to be done to* or even "done in" by others and by ourselves.

Everyone created, directly and immediately, by an *infinitely* pure act of being (God), must be perfect: must be an act that is finite, but pure. Every original gift of being—every person—is simply a *purely active* potency: a being that is *capable of doing perfectly everything in its giftedly-unique power of be-ing.*

"Pure" should not necessarily mean *infinite*. Our tradition has been conflating the pure and the infinite. We have never contemplated how *we* must *be* finitely pure acts of created being. Still, *as divinely gifted*, that is what we *are*.

The Pure Act of Being That We Were Gifted to Be

In creation *ex nihilo*, every person is gifted to *be permanently a finite pure act of be*-ing. God *cannot* possibly create—directly out of nothing—beings that are even slightly defective and that have any *passive* potency, *and still be God.*

Created persons are *perfect as gifted*, though multitudes of us—the ones who come to planet earth—are *imperfect as received, because of the faltering way we received the gift of our being.* God said *Be*, and *we*—the eventual inhabitants of space and time—must have said, immediately and freely, *maybe. We* determined ourselves to be the *kind* of *human* persons we *are* as a whole—quite imperfect ones.

We were indecisive. So, as the result of even a slight hesitation to *be* the finite being with which we were gifted, we fell into the passivity of darkness. What else could have happened? We made ourselves kinds of being that are 'here and now,' 'there and then.' As a result, we are not so much *be*-ings as *may-be*-ings. *Maybe* we'll see tomorrow or, at least, a minute more. *May-be* we won't.

Yet we are still free. Our freedom is seriously passivized, but not gone. We can *actively* receive these wounded and recovering beings of ours. We are not just passive. We have the active power to receive—to receive revelation from nature and from God. We can acknowledge having said *maybe* and thereby having numbed our being. And we can be sorry for that *originative* sin and, as well, be sorry that we blame God unconsciously for inheriting the sin of our first parents. We can take God "off the hook." Unconsciously, as well as consciously.

Perhaps, we can also take *us* off the hook—the hook of excuses that pose as reasons. Why do bad things happen to good people? We *know* why, in the depths of our unconscious, self-benumbed being. We know we are not as good as we might *think* we are. That is why, in the midst of our joyful hope, we might shrink when we think about our origins.

Chapter 6

Let's Stop Blaming God

Once and for all, let's stop blaming God. We will be able to stop if we submit ourselves to some critical questions. And if our answers are honest. These questions and answers provide an understanding of *why* we inherited original sin and why God is not to blame for it.

The Major Questions

First of all, is God really *infinitely* good? Or something other than infinite in goodness? If God is not infinitely good, just how good *is* God?

A less-than-infinite God might be called 'a god,' but not God. No being with goodness that is other than infinite can be the gifter of any goodness-at-all. No being that is other than *eternal* (infinite being, without beginning or end) can render, from nothing, any being at all. No purely finite being—however good, admirable, and loving—can be responsible for there being any being-at-all or any goodness-at-all.

Perfect *finite* goodness can indeed *be*. But it cannot ultimately be the source of itself, much less the source of any other goodness. A created being is limited to being an absolutely *receiving* kind of being, and one that is only *so* good or *so* powerful—however good or however powerful. In a perfect *finite* being there could be no *absolutely* originative, creating power. Created persons, angelic and human, cannot create anything out of nothing.

Secondly, anyone who affirms God's being as infinitely good, is faced with the next question. Is God really *infinitely* powerful (able to do whatever is doable—whatever is not contradictory—and to act with *unlimited* effectiveness and wisdom)? Or is God something other than infinite in power? If God is not infinitely powerful, how powerful is God; and is this being really God?

Divine power is not a "power-over us" so much as an infinite power-*with* us. (It is, of course, not at all a power *of* us.) This power is *infinitely with* us, without being our own power. Only our own lack of actively receiving our *own* being has us thinking that God's power is limited and that it is only a power "over" us. Sadly, we do not receive God's infinite intimacy. We fear intimacy with the infinite. And why would we not? Our fear strongly suggests that we somehow know the depth of our self-chosen emptiness.

In our own times, Rabbi Harold Kushner has presented God as being limited in power (*When Bad Things Happen to Good People*: Avon, 1983). He and millions of readers, however, are sadly mistaken. They abandon the Judeo-Christian meaning of God as *both* infinitely good *and* infinitely powerful. It is *unreasonable*, however, to hold that God is infinitely good, and then to think that this infinite goodness is not *matched* by a *power* that is infinite. The unlimited power of infinite goodness and the unlimited goodness of infinite power are given little notice. The problem *seems* to be *why* the so-called, all-good God cannot prevent evil from befalling "perfectly innocent children" and even adults whose infirmities keep them 'incapable of sin.'

But the basic impediment actually resides in people's inability to *mean* infinite when they hear or use the term. Many really seem to mean indefinite, rather than infinite. God is then thought to be *infinitely* good and *indefinitely* powerful, but not infinitely *powerful*.

Often Christians and other theists employ the terms omnipotent (all-powerful), omniscient, and omnibenevolent in referring to God. But this grossly misleads. God is not really God, if merely all-good and all-powerful. The "all" necessarily signifies something or someone who is finite: limited in goodness and power. But the living God of genuine theism is unlimitedly good and unlimitedly powerful. *No* limits.

It is easy to confuse the infinite with the indefinite, as happens when mathematicians postulate an "infinite number." Mathematical numbers, however, might better be called *indefinite*, since the very *being* of numbers and of quantity is finite. The *kind* of being of these elements of passive matter is utterly finite. Not knowing what the *actual* limits are, we can still know *that* there *are* actual limits to the whole field of the quantified and numerical. In mathematics, rooted in the workings of the quantitative imagination, bereft of qualities, "infinite" means indefinite. In reality, infinite means God.

I suspect that unconsciously we do not *want* God to be *infinite actuality* in goodness and in power. We could no longer be content, then, to think of God manipulatively, albeit subconsciously, where we can, as it were, control God *in our own minds*. We are constantly projecting onto God our functionalistic propensities. We are strongly inclined to think that God must act, in our own image and likeness, as a kind of mega-creature.

For instance, we can readily mistake the friendship of God. We can think of God as a kind of big buddy. God is felt to be our pal who will never abandon us and who will condescend to approve of our motives and actions, despite their inadequacies, very much like our companions on earth. In the long run, we think God will come around. For us, it is easy to live with the idea that *mean-ing* always begins with *me*. Even the meaning for God.

We are unconsciously trying to block even the slightest awareness of the depths of our alienation. At the invitation of the three Infinite Persons, "Be, and be-*with* Us," we partly declined to *be*. Thus, we did not desire to be a *perfectly finite* being. We *somewhat* wanted to be another Person of God—as it were, a kind of 'fourth person of the Blessed Trinity.'

We *could* not, of course, at the moment of creation *ex nihilo*, stop God from *gifting* us with *being*—the perfect, giving side of the gift. But, by our reticent *yes/no*, we could and did muddle the gift, on its receiving side. So, we are now both perfect and imperfect persons. Perfect forever, *as gifted by God*. But, as received by ourselves, imperfect for now, and possibly, even grossly imperfect forever, if we do not *fully receive* redemption and attain our salvation.

Theology and the Two Creations

What we did at the *non-durational* instant of creation is the *cause* of our present personal predicament: living in this fragile, largely chaotic, world. Immediately, we gave an imperfect reception—*of* our being *by* our being. We made ourselves mediocre kinds of being. When God said, "Be," we must have said, "Maybe." (So to say, "Let me think about it!" God gave us *plenty* of space and time to do just that. Consider the starry heavens and the aging of the earth. Consider the galaxies of galaxies and the eons of existence.) We are now living out our *yes/no* to God and to our God-gifted being. Here within the confines of space and time, at our conception, we must have inherited our own *beingfully* originative sin. But the inheriting was transmitted *in and through* the *historically* original sin of Adam and Eve that we also inherited.

Theologians today seem to be hung up on creation as a *process*—whether lasting six days or six eons. But there is nothing perfect about a process. God's originative creation could *not* possibly *be* a process. Thinking so constitutes a blight, both on the theology of a six-day creation and on the theology of theistic evolution. Both creationism and theistic evolution overlook the *orginatively* original creation. Often, they think they are referring to creation *ex nihilo*. But they are really talking about *redemptive* creation—creation *ex aliquo, out of something*: out of chaos, darkness, dust, gametes, or the like.

A critical distinction must be made between the two kinds of divine creation: creation 'out of nothing' (surmised mainly through critical analysis in philosophy and theology) and the creation 'out of *something*' (as in the *Book of Genesis*, whether understood literally or figuratively). Otherwise, we will continue doing the treadmill on creation. We will definitely be blaming God unconsciously for *directly* creating us as imperfect creatures at our conception within our mothers. Surely, as Jews, Christians, and other sensitive people, we can understand in a better way.[1]

Everyone who thinks that *Genesis* has the last word on creation out of *nothing* is missing the meaning of an *originative* sin that is the subject of spiritual repression. As *infinitely* good and *infinitely* powerful, God could not possibly let Adam and Eve or anyone else impose their sin upon other persons: no matter how good the 'ultimate consequences' would seem to be. Not even for the sake of an ecstatic reward in heaven forever. Infinite Goodness could never

---

[1] A much fuller response is given in my trilogy entitled, *When God Said Be, We Said Maybe: An Inside Story of the Creation, the Crash, and the Recovery of Being* (LifeCom 2010). Volume one serves as a basic introduction: *God Said, We Said: The Interpersonal Act of Creation.* (170 pp.) Volume two elaborates at length: *God Says, We Say: The Interpersonal Act of Redemption.* (289 pp.) Volume three intensifies and concludes: *God Will Say, We Will Say: The Interpersonal Act of Salvation.* (255 pp.) Volumes two and three combine to include about 75 pages with 57 Questions and Responses on the new worldview for theists. All three volumes include an extensive glossary. These books can be ordered through Amazon.com, Barnesandnoble.com, Lifemeaning.com, and other sources.

do evil that a so-called "greater good" might result. Thinking in that utilitarian way, consciously or unconsciously, as the whole tradition of human culture has done, demeans God. Adam and Eve could not inflict us with their sin unless we had already been self-wounded and able to be imposed upon. So, why blame them?

Chapter 7

Let's Stop Blaming Adam and Eve

Let's distract ourselves. That seems to be what believers have said through the ages. They know the facts from *Genesis*. They also have a vague idea of what creation *out of nothing* must have entailed. But the question is difficult. We find it almost impossible to "think about" our perfect creation and its cause—an infinitely perfect kind of being. And also, to consider that we had perfect freedom to be instantly with God forever! Ah, but we can *know* that it is true.

Tragically, in the last few centuries, theologians have developed an excellent "shield" against becoming aware of how we blame Adam and Eve unconsciously for the prime origin of *our* sin. They rationalize how we all must have come into existence from these "first parents" through *evolution.*

Even were some forms of evolution true, it could only be because of one thing: the way *we* had immediately and freely responded to God at the moment of our creation *out of nothing.* And it had nothing to do with evolution. We must have hesitated to *be*, and to be the *created* kind of being that the divine Persons were gifting us to be. Living in space and time, whether evolutional or not, is strictly remedial. We need mega-rehabilitation, individually and communally.

At the instant of creation, we balked at being *limitedly* perfect. At least to some degree, we wanted immediately to be *infinitely* perfect. In desiring to be so, our own self-determining be-ing crashed into itself and created passive potency—the condition of having to be "done to." Immediately, we faced the challenge of be-*coming*: being *coming* back from the unimaginable fall—or rather from a plunge—that we freely initiated. Our be-ing remained ontologically comatose for ages. From within that primitive condition of be-*coming*, starting with *Genesis*, God redeems us and is now trying to save us.

It is no wonder that there are atheists. Along with most theists, they have become fixated upon this fallen, struggling world of recovery that is all around us and within us. Thereby, many folks think we can quite logically surmise that God is neither all-powerful nor all-good. God allows all of us to be hit with the 'sin of Adam'— somebody else's sin. We then wobble around here in conditions of sin, where it is inevitable that we succumb all the more. The many devious arguments of the atheists and agnostics seem reinforced by the tortures and sufferings of multitudes of 'innocent little children.'

What, then, is the basic response to those who say that—in the face of these enormous evils and horrendous injustice—the "all-knowing, all-powerful, and all-good" God could not possibly exist?

Does God Exist?

First of all, we can reply that they are right. God does not *ex*-ist. God *is*. People are still trying to understand God by ordinary human conceptualization—still trying to *grasp* God, as it were, in their own minds. And then, within the narrow confines of defective human reasoning, they try to hold on and spin it. They try to *grasp* at the *idea* of God, or even at the *being* of God, and end up with little meaning.

God is known, however, but not by grasping. The *being* of God does not exist; and therefore cannot be seized. The *being* of God simply *is* and *is known*, even though the knowers might not consciously admit—nor want to admit—they *are always knowing* God. At least, unconsciously and preconsciously. For the infinite Being, *to be is to be known*, if not loved, by all persons—the attentive, the rejecting, and the indifferent. Satanic forces *know* God.

Existence is not the same as *being*. Regrettably, philosophers and theologians in the Judeo-Christian tradition have overlooked the basic difference between existence and being. They often fail to notice the difference between the *way* finite, defective kinds of being *are* and the *way* perfect beings *are*: whether perfect infinitely or finitely.

Practically, yet largely unconsciously, existence means to stand (*sistere*) outside of (*ex*). But there is nothing like an inside/outside to complete *being*. Inside/outside applies basically to those beings that *exist*: existents. Existing beings are really beings that are extended in some way. They are 'outside themselves' in some manner. They are not simply be-ings. They exist as *affected* beings—as not entirely genuine.

There are basically two kinds of existents. One kind *stands outside* self physically. This kind has extension or dimension, such as trees and water drops and all other physical things. The other kind stands outside self spiritually and mentally. These beings are reflectively conscious beings, namely humans, who are not only conscious, but also self-conscious. That is, we humans are *able* to be conscious of our *consciousness* of things. We are unlike higher organisms that are *simply* conscious or aware—sensorily and immediately, and often keenly. A human person can know not only the tree, but can know his or her *knowing* of the tree. A bird or other animal, no matter how perceptive the awareness, cannot ever know self as *self* or know its very *knowing* activities themselves. And birds know trees, but not *as* trees, that is, as to *what* they are or *why* they are.

So, fallen humans, animals, plants, stones, and all the particles of matter have a manner of being that we call *existing*. Fallen humans, however, are persons (complete beings) who are able to know and love themselves and others—or to know and hate themselves and others. And they not only *be*; they *exist* in both basic manners. They exist as extended material beings and as self-reflective knowers. We fallen humans who are compromised, do *extend* ourselves, both materially and spiritually. We exist in this world, but we do so outside ourselves within ourselves: *put here by our originative willingness, at the first moment of being, to be "more than" who we are*.

This is why God *could* not stop the Holocaust *even by infinite power*. At the absolutely free moment of creation out of nothing, God had gifted to every one of those who would be victims, 'later,' in space and time, the perfect power to prevent cosmic existence from happening to them in the first place. The same was gifted to everyone else. Sad to say, we can be certain that all fallen humans who inhabit the earth are necessarily susceptible to every manner of evil that can happen during their cosmic existence.

By saying a *full yes* to God and to our own be-ing, we would have escaped temporal suffering, and even the unimaginable possibility of horrendous suffering in hell forever. We had perfect finite freedom to receive, fully and immediately, the gift of being-*with* God forever. (And if we deny such, we are denying either that God is infinitely good *or* that God is infinitely powerful—or both.)

Human Suffering and Compassion

As it is now, we are vulnerable to experiencing a holocaust in this world—a kind of hell on earth. As individuals and as groups, we are susceptible. Yes, we need to try to do whatever we can to console and support victims of the past and of the present, and to prevent such enormities from ever happening again. That is, we have been commanded to love our neighbor as ourselves.

But we should also come to *acknowledge* in our lives the ultimate source of *all* brutality, indifference, suffering, and death. We each meet that enemy daily in every mirror. As the old saying has it, we *are* our own worst enemy.

If we are honest, we will also see that God cannot go against God with respect to power and goodness. God's infinite goodness-and-power *infinitely respects* our finite goodness and power and *could* not "bail us out." A creator who would act like that could only be finite *and defective*. But, by limitless love and respect for personal freedom, God exercises *infinitely potent* restraint. God is unlimitedly receptive—not necessarily approving—of our being and our doing. God's infinite freedom allows us our finite freedom to its maximum.

Miraculous interventions are included in God's infinite freedom that allows for our finite freedom. A deep, hidden well of good will within any of us might result in God's infinite and abiding power being able to create something 'outside the order of nature.' God can stop the effects of adversity upon us, but only because *we* have somehow rendered ourselves open to a miracle and are able to receive God's infinite mercy.

By ignorance of personal, originative sin and by our consequent arrogance of self-promotion, we are able to doubt or even deny the *being* of God. We have been amazingly inclined to demand that God *be* the way *we* want *being* to be. Consequently, we *unconsciously avoid* the issue of *originative* sin and our repression of it—blinded as we are by that self-originative sin itself. That very sin tends to block us from becoming aware of it.

We who are apt to label God a 'monster' for "choosing not to stop atrocities" need a much deeper meaning for *be*-ing. Then we might come to find that *we* are the monsters, who are desperately in need of unprecedented repentance. Adolph Hitler has been dubbed the scourge of God. But he was only one of the extremely outrageous members of our own "*maybe* family."

When we mainly blame someone like Hitler, or even Satan, for the malicious evils that we experience or anticipate, we are inevitably also blaming God, whom we know allows it. And we reveal our smallness of mind and heart. This constriction of our self-concept could have been caused only by ourselves in our originative sin—committed *with* Adam and Eve and multitudes of others.

We can meaningfully receive the fate we endure in this contingent, *maybe* world, where good and evil are thoroughly mixed. Our very deployment here is the gracious gift of God, called redemption, including a final hope of salvation and everlasting friendship.

Here and now, we are redeemed, but not yet saved. We have multitudes of crucial choices to make. These include especially our choices of *attitude*. To be God's friend is to receive actively—in attitude and action—what is truly good.

Changing the Attitude of Making-Excuses

We have an inveterate tendency to blame circumstances and other people for our problems, mishaps, and misfortunes. Even many devout persons are inclined to blame the devil first. They do not realize how they had already put themselves in the presence of evil by their attitude toward be-ing, just as Adam and Eve did "well before" the experience of temptation in the Garden.

By the mercifulness of redemption, we have been rescued from this momentous fracture in our being. But only so far. We have been traveling on the way to completing our final self-determination: either being *with* God in heaven or *against* God in hell. It is *not* 'all up to God.' It is all up to you and me. Whatever determination and acts of freedom are yet to transpire will come from us in the ever-present light of God's never-failing grace.

We were redeemed and sustained without our conscious consent. But God cannot save us, even with infinite power, if we do not *cooperate* by receiving our God-gifted freedom and by giving our consent always to do *God's* will, and never simply our own.

Calling God our Savior is good, but not enough. We must *prove our sincerity* in claiming Jesus or God as our Savior. Sincerity certifies our friendship. Without Faith, none of our works are worth anything. They cannot earn us one whit of salvation-value. But neither do our claims to be saved, if they are somehow insincere— consciously or unconsciously. We can show our sincerity by good-willed efforts at virtue that reveals sincerity, not worthiness.

Not everyone who says, "Lord, Lord," really intends it. Self-deception is quite possible. Constant prayer and offering our lives to God's work are needed. Self-deception was involved in the very first act of our being, in the moment of being created out of nothing. We deceived ourselves. And we can readily do it again and again.

Indeed, no one can be deceived by another—including Satan— without having first deceived himself or herself. And the ability of someone to deceive us in anything comes from our already having made ourselves self-deceivable.

No work of ours can save us, except the "work" of sincere belief in the life of Jesus. Our sincerity takes work. Or, if we have never had the message sincerely presented, it is necessary that we are willing to believe—at least unconsciously—in Jesus Christ as our Savior.

If we move ourselves as best we can to do God's will until death, we can come to know that "Eye has not seen nor ear heard nor has it entered into the human heart, what God has prepared for those who love him" (1 *Corinthians* 2:9). But if we blow off life as a fun scene or as some amazing cosmic escape from profound responsibility for our actions and our be-ing, we will know the ultimate effects of our unconscious desires: rather than love God with our *whole* heart, we would prefer to experience hell forever. And that subconsciously-willed destiny is a far worse outcome than millions of years in Auschwitz. It is a destiny far from wanted; but by our supremely free (finite) ability to will what we will (to love or to hate), such can be willed. Many would prefer to hate God forever, rather than admit God's sovereignty.

So, those who experienced the Holocaust of the 1940's, or any other horror on the earth, can hardly complain *before God*. As an expression of their enraged, dispirited emotional lives, however, complaints are inevitable. Complaints witness to the incredible injustice perpetrated on them by their fellow human beings, who are quite obviously sinners at heart. We need to admit our feelings and deepest emotions. We also need to *own* them, and then to be compassionate toward ourselves and others. But we will only become free of sour emotions *by taking ourselves off the hook of the excuses we are inclined to make*.

Horrible happenings like the Holocaust should announce to us our own originative sin—the sin that each one of us has committed in full freedom. These primal transgressions transcend any temptation-induced sin, such as that of Adam and Eve in Eden. Originative sin is the primal cause of the historical chain of sin called original.

When bad incidents happen to us, we tend to blame Joe or Jane, as a way of excusing ourselves. Even if the happening was specifically the fault of someone else, it is *always our fault that it happened to us at all.* We could have been in heaven, but are now experiencing the faults of many others, ultimately and only, because we originally said *maybe* to our own act of be-ing. The "fault line" goes back, through Adam and Eve, to our originative sin.

So, as "justifiable outrage" at the living God, our protests signify a profound deficiency in understanding our true condition. Often such protests constitute a degree of ill will that is held in common with the perpetrators of the outrageous deeds done *to* us.

Rebellion against God because of the Auschwitz experience sadly testifies to the distance our minds have moved from the core of genuine Judeo-Christian belief. Pain, suffering, starvation, and every imaginable kind of torture have been visited upon God's children on earth. Why should any of God's chosen people—Jews, Christians, and others—be excepted? They should rather be exceptional. Not in being spared, but in the way they receive their treatment as being repentant souls, anticipating fully the mercy of God in their lives later, if not sooner—in eternity, if not also in time.

If we were let off *entirely*, without any punishment at all, God would be simply a monster of injustice. If even one sinner were to live a life of paradisal bliss—with nothing except joy and pleasure, devoid of any sorrow or pain—God *would be* unjust. Not so much unjust to the rest of us, but to that sinner himself or herself. God is infinitely good and just, and *could* not violate divine Nature and the inherent consequences of our freedom by totally preventing personal sin's effects to take place.

Our very *existence in this world* is a kind of punishment. And if we ever came to realize radically *why* we are planted *here*, we might be mortified and might even say, "Oh, so that's what happened."

By our primal sin, we made ourselves dull to the infinite dignity of the One offended. Understandably, then, we become defensive at the indignities committed against ourselves and against multitudes of our companions on the planet earth. Yet we somehow know that the offenders are violating the divine-like nature of human beings and the divine goodness itself.

Unfortunately, we are inclined to *overlook the roots*: the primal reality of *originative* sin and the practically equal violation done to God by the victims, the perpetrators, and the viewers of the atrocities. By our *either-or* mindedness, we deceive ourselves into thinking that the vicious propagators of extreme violence are the "bad guys" and the victims are the "good guys." But if we took to heart more deeply the whole of the Judeo-Christian tradition, we could see and speak with a new *both-and* mindedness. We would realize that, while the violators remain much more reprehensible than the victims *in the instances at hand*, *both* the violators *and* the victims are ultimately originative sinners. Who would dare, then, to make individual assessments of the consequences of each person's particular degree of responsibility, right at the core of its origin?

Once we come to realize the *both-and* truth of the matter, we can become disposed to forgive our enemies and our persecutors, in the way Jesus commanded. Without such realization, we necessarily, if largely unconsciously, blame God for both our predicaments and our punishments. We think, why did *God* allow me to get trapped in these situations? We do not think, why did *I* ever say less than fully *yes* to God in full freedom at the very beginning of my being? When severe suffering occurs, we think numbly, why *me*, rather than: why *not* me.

God Will Provide, But We Will Decide

Apparently, not even the Biblical character, Job, thought to ask this poignant question, why *not* me? It suggests to most people a kind of masochism. Jewish, Christian, and other traditions might seem to have avoided it systematically.

But rare individuals have, on occasion, learned to live well with the question. Cindi Broaddus is one example in our own time.

In the blackness of night, June 5, 2001, she experienced her own personally painful wake-up call. She and a companion were about to drive under an Oklahoma freeway overpass. Suddenly, a jar of acid crashed through the windshield and burned them. Cindi received a nearly death-dealing affliction. Later, she suffered excruciatingly painful kinds of treatment and massive skin-grafting throughout a period of many months. She recovered rather well and was able to tell her heroic story to millions on the *Dr. Phil Show*, the *Hour of Power*, and other programs. Her incomparable confidence in God's goodness, as well as her love for family, friends, neighbors, and strangers, eventually opened her heart to the unknown assailant.

At one point, Cindi's suffering reached a spiritual climax. Finally, she broke away from hating another person and what he had done to her. She came to realize that she had been hating the person *she had become* in asking, "Why me?" The turnaround question struck her: "Why *not* me?" She started to hate what she had *allowed* her physical, emotional, and social hurts to do to *her*.

In her compelling book, *A Random Act*, Cindi tells her experience. Her dramatic change in perspective has even prompted the social movement known as committing random acts of kindness. She hopes that her still-unknown assailant, along with millions of others, will one day receive such acts. The random act of violence done to Cindi has occasioned the spreading message of people doing random acts of kindness every day. Cindi's powerful change of heart became the specific cause of spreading goodness and self-sacrificial love— the only authentic kind for human persons in being redeemed.

We need to receive a new freedom and joy by helping those who are victims of an oppression that would seem to be even greater than ours. We have abundant reason to struggle for justice that integrates the human with the divine. We can become grateful to God for redeeming *all* of us. We also *will* to receive this infinite Love, and to *act* on it. There is no room in the fully repentant heart for even the partial denial of the saving, infinite power of God. We need to bring out the truth about the saving, finite power of a *sincerely* repentant heart. Our *possible* hatred of God may be unconscious now. So, acts of conscious love will be required to bring to light our potential for union with God.

Again, let's stop blaming—consciously and unconsciously—Adam and Eve, as well as infinite Goodness. Let's really cease projecting our self-constituted weakness onto God's unlimited Love.

Instead, we can begin to make much greater efforts to swim, with loving self-sacrifice, against the current of human misery, found within the river flooding into every human life. When we reach the headwaters of this massive flow, we will be able to admit our repressed presence there, at the origin of our *be*-ing, where even now we encounter, largely unconsciously, but really, the living God.

We are now able to live more and more from the perfect side of our God-gifted being. The more we affirm God as the Gifter of the perfect side of our being, the more we can live in real trust that God's infinite love will save us. But the more we refrain from our being-*with* the God-side, the less we can be confident in salvation. God has done God's infinitely powerful part. Will we actively believe? Will we actively receive?

Even though they might not agree, non-Christian believers in God can appreciate the reason Christians recap their Faith by quoting a particular passage of Scripture. "God so loved the world that He gave His only begotten Son" (*John* 3:16). Perhaps, that is where, eventually, all can come somehow to discern that the heart of God is bleeding from our root-sins. And only through this Blood of the suffering of God, streaking through the river of human misery can we be fully cleansed and gloriously saved.

Afterward

Deepening Our Faith

This book presents a critical choice. Faithful Christians and other theists can continue to believe in the ways of thinking about creation and sin that they have been taught. Or they can believe what they have been taught, but with significant enhancement of its meaning.

Does "creation out of nothing" suggest that God first created darkness, chaos, and waters over the earth, and then inserted light, vegetation, animal organisms, and humankind *out of nothing*? Was creation, first of all, a series of finite moves on God's part, forming creatures serially in one *immense process*? Or was original creation an infinite act, creating *only finite persons*—angels and humans, all at once—with some of them responding fully positive, some fully negative. And did others respond *both* positively *and* negatively to some degree or other, leaving the "dusty results," from which begins the *Genesis* story of Adam and Eve?

The choice is either to reject the new hypothesis or to consider it seriously as deepening the understanding of things already believed.

The new being-theology, sketched within this volume, offers a potentially deeper perspective on time-tested truths of Faith. The reader can relate to the old and the new accounts with an either-or mind or a both-and mind. One can say, "The new view is either right or wrong and is opposed to the older view." Or one can think that both interpretations can be true and that the newer simply attempts to affirm and to expand the older perspective.

Both views present where we came from and where we are going in a manner that is understandable. The traditional assessment seems simpler and easier to follow. It is familiar. But the second version gives enhanced background on the basic truths—a background that is quite true or not so true, as time and theological discussion will prove.

The choice is unavoidable. In closing this book, the reader faces, consciously and unconsciously, the differences. The two views will be seen as either contradictory or simply contrasting, with the newer view being either a development or a diminishment of the traditional view.

In any event, I would like to ask whether you really think that the *Book of Genesis* begins at the very beginning? If you think so, where is the creation of the angels to be found? Already, in chapter three, a spiritual presence, a tempter, is revealed. Creation of the angels *ex nihilo* seems to be presumed.

From the form of a serpent, the fallen angel's voice is heard in the Garden. "God knows that if you eat of it, you shall become as Gods, knowing good and evil" (*Gen.* 3:5). This commanding intimidation reveals a creature with power who is ready to pounce spiritually upon Adam and Eve, the naïve couple who were enjoying their newfound pleasures, while obviously looking for more. Where did this serpentine threat come from? *Genesis* does not say.

The threat surely did not come from God's infinite goodness. This tantalizing inclination to choose evil was already present in Adam and Eve *before* they sinned by succumbing to *temptation*. Satan took advantage of a weakness already there.

Obviously, *Genesis* does not start at the primal beginning. Divine revelation, after all, proclaims without necessarily explaining. Receivers of this Revelation, wanting to understand it better, need to explore the inexhaustible meaning that resides *within* its message.

The physical conditions of the chaos and the darkness, along with the tempter's spiritually evil momentum of ill-will toward God, speak volumes about the dubiously moral status of Adam and Eve *before* their *historically* original sin. Adam spoke with God, and was in God's company, but hardly as an ecstatic friend. In Eden, Adam and Eve had already fallen by abusing their pristine state of freedom in their first *act* of freedom, the act of imperfectly exercising this perfect freedom power. They were thereby weak and temptable.

Apparently, there is a missing background to the story in *Genesis*: a reality that precedes any 'telling of a spatiotemporal story.' Why does this latent backstory not appear at the creation of Adam from dust and of Eve from Adam's rib? Or, as in the first lines of *Genesis*, how could God start with darkness, chaos and a void over the deep? God creates *ex nihilo* only spiritual light, from which darkness or chaos comes *only by those who badly receive* the light.

Sincere believers want a compelling account of what happened to Adam before he was created (or re-habilitated) out of dust—out of something lowly. The analysis in the present book indicates that something profoundly weakening had to have occurred.

If you agree that something big about the beginning of human existence is missing, this book about a perfect creation could help you throw back the curtain and look freshly into the light.

Theology is a continuous enterprise. It attempts to make sense out of the sacred Revelation, gifted to us through Scripture, Tradition, and the teaching authority of the Church. The Spirit of God teaches through these avenues and others, including the structure of nature, both physical and spiritual. Today, many Christians are engaged in what they call the new evangelization, a huge task of reconverting the fallen-away, as well as those who never knew Christ. To bring back many and to present the Faith more vigorously to all, they need meanings for sin that is deeper than the traditional. Some of the old meanings for creation and the origin of evil are less than plausible.

Over the centuries, mortal men and women have tried to focus on the voice of God, so that people may hear better and believe more in clarity and depth, the better to hope more and love more.

Longing for progress, Pope John Paul II called for a kind of new springtime in theology. In his Encyclical on *Faith and Reason* in 1998, he called specifically for philosophers of *being* to provide critical input for the understanding of the faith.

> The *intellectus fidei*…demands the contribution of a philosophy of being which…would enable dogmatic theology to perform its functions appropriately…. It must turn to the philosophy of being, which should be able anew to propose the problem of being…without lapsing into sterile repetition of antiquated formulas. Set within the Christian metaphysical tradition, the philosophy of being is a dynamic philosophy which views reality in its ontological, causal and communicative structures. It is strong and enduring because it is based upon the very act of being itself, which allows a full and comprehensive openness to reality as a whole, surpassing every limit in order to reach the One who brings all things to fulfillment.

(*Fides et Ratio*, no. 97)

I have tried to respond seriously to that theological urgency and to bring believers into the relatively unexplored backstory of creation in *Genesis*. In that promising context, we can attempt to make more sense out of what Christians and others are affirming—implicitly, if not explicitly—on God, creation, and sin. Knowing ourselves as *acts* of human *be*-ing can be helpful and perhaps even necessary.

The book starts with *being*, stays with *being*, and ends with *being*. This perspective of ultimate significance is thereby able to reach deeper into the roots of Faith. The traditional mindset moves from the naturalistic (cosmological) to the rationalistic (metaphysical) to the specifically theological, without seeing everything and everyone primarily in their *being*. The immediate and lasting ontological level of discourse in the new being-theology makes human thought ready to blend better with Revelation.

The content of thought does not spin away from Church teaching, as gnostic and elitist forays of explanation have done historically. Every Christian and every theist of sound mind and sound teaching can follow what this book is saying and meaning, if they *will* to do so. The work does not rely on the imagination, but on the dynamics of natural and supernatural reasoning. The book is intended to be a deepening and an enrichment of our knowing, the better to believe that God is *always infinite* in love, mercy, goodness, and power— and that by our own perfect, God-gifted freedom we can say, fully and perfectly, *yes* to God forever.

*****

About the Author

Robert E. Joyce, PhD, *professor emeritus* of philosophy at St. John's University, Collegeville, Minnesota is the author of various books and numerous articles in scholarly and popular publications. He published, with Mary Rosera Joyce, *Let Us Be Born* (Chicago: Franciscan Herald Press, 1970), the first paperback in the prolife movement. In the same year, Mary and Robert published their unique introduction to the philosophy of man and woman, *New Dynamics in Sexual Love: A Revolutionary Approach to Marriage and Celibacy* (Collegeville, MN: St. John's University Press, 1970). Robert's doctoral dissertation was published in 1980 by University Press of America. Parts of *Human Sexual Ecology: A Philosophy and Ethics of Man and Woman* have been used in University courses and by several leaders in the natural family planning movement.

His latest books include *Affirming Our Freedom in God: The Untold Story of Creation; Facing the Dark Side of Genesis: A New Understanding of Ourselves; A Perfect Creation: Light on the Dark Side of Genesis;* and *The Origin of Pain and Evil.*

In 2010, the author published a trilogy. It includes

God Said, We Said: The Interpersonal Act of Creation

God Says, We Say: The Interpersonal Act of Redemption

God Will Say, We Will Say: The Interpersonal Act of Salvation

Human Life and Sexuality Series

Along with others, this book by Mary Rosera Joyce:

The Future of Adam and Eve: Finding the Lost Gift

(LifeCom, 2009) 267 pages

Adam's Puritan-Playboy America; True Sexual Freedom; Friendship; Sexual Likeness to God; True Feminism; Sexuality and the Trinity; the Meaning of Personhood; the Origin of Evil; *et al.*

Two Creations Series

The following three books by Robert E. Joyce form a trilogy called: *When God Said Be, We Said Maybe: An Inside Story of the Creation, the Crash, and the Recovery of Being*

God Said, We Said: The Interpersonal Act of Creation (LifeCom 2010) 170 pages. Glossary. First book in the trilogy.

God Says, We Say: The Interpersonal Act of Redemption (LifeCom 2010) 290 pages. Includes many Qs and As. Glossary. Second book in the trilogy.

God Will Say, We Will Say: The Interpersonal Act of Salvation (LifeCom 2010) 256 pages. Includes many Qs and As. Glossary. Third book in the trilogy.

In addition to these books, there are others by R. E. Joyce:

Affirming Our Freedom in God:
        The Untold Story of Creation
(LifeCom, 2001) 100 pages.

The Cry of Why, beneath the Holocaust; Are We Hiding Something? God Freely Creates Our Freedom to Create, *et al.*

Facing the Dark Side of Genesis:
        A New Understanding of Ourselves
(LifeCom, 2008) 84 pages.

The Genesis Gap; Originative Sin; Theology of the Person's Being; Two Creations: Originative and Redemptive; Consequences for a Life of Faith, *et al.*

A Perfect Creation: The Light behind the Dark Side of Genesis
(LifeCom, 2008) 170 pages.

From Cosmess to Cosmos; The Missing Infinity of God; God's
Intimate Act of Creation; The Meaning of Evil and Its Cause, *et al*.

The Origin of Pain and Evil
(LifeCom, 2008) 40 pages

Why Blame Adam and Eve? How We Did It to Ourselves
(LifeCom, 2014) 77 pages

**All of the books above are available at Amazon.com,
Barnesandnoble.com, and other outlets, as well as by order
through any bookstore, or from *LifeCom*.**

Booklet available through *LifeCom*:

*New Light within the Christian Worldview:
Clarification on Creation and the Origin of Evil*
(LifeCom, 2011) 35 pages

The new Creation Theory summarized for scholars and pastors.

LifeCom
Box 1832, St. Cloud, MN 56302
Lifemeaning.com

www.ingramcontent.com/pod-product-compliance
Lightning Source LLC
Chambersburg PA
CBHW021218020426
42331CB00003B/371